Fasten
Your
Seatbelts

FASTEN YOUR SEATBELTS

A FLIGHT ATTENDANT'S ADVENTURES
36,000 FEET AND BELOW

BY CHRISTINE CHURCHILL

ISBN: 0615757731
ISBN-13: 9780615757735
Library of Congress Control Number: 2013931169

Gonos Publishing Company
Vero Beach, FL

Some of the names have been changed to protect the innocent and the not so innocent.

Cataloging

Churchill, Christine.
Fasten Your Seatbelts:
A Flight Attendant's Adventures 36,000 Feet and Below.

Edited by: Patrick McCoy

2014 First Edition

Dedication

This book is dedicated to the pilots who have flown me and hundreds of thousands of passengers safely from one destination to another and to my fellow flight attendants whom I cherish like my own family.

To my loving husband who has been supportive of this book and the airline lifestyle for these many years. His computer skills were priceless.

Lastly, I want to thank my parents for their unconditional love and for taking me to the airport when I was a little girl. They planted in me the thirst for adventure and the seeds of a dream.

Contents

Introduction

$\mathscr{F}$ulfilling, exciting, terrifying and humbling best describes my career as a flight attendant. Despite the many changes in the airline industry, I still love to fly. I enjoy sharing the events of my countless trips around the world with other crewmembers, family and friends and have been told time and time again, "You need to write a book."

These stories are all true and occurred both on and off the aircraft. They are told to the best of my memory and portray my life and career in chronological order. Flight attendants are required to attend annual emergency training classes. We discuss actual emergencies and train for potential ones. I realized over the years that I have already experienced a good portion of those incidents. Fellow crewmembers jokingly say, "Hey, I don't want to fly with you; you get in too many situations!"

I have participated in some very memorable and frightening events: decompression, unconscious passengers, critical low fuel situations, severe turbulence, lost hydraulics and all types of emergencies, heartbreak and hijinks on and off the ground. So, I am not surprised when I hear these comments!

Of course, when I share the escapades of international flying, the wonderful and not so pleasant layovers, unforgettable characters and all the fun and scintillating times with crewmembers and passengers, their reservations are quickly dispelled! All I ask of you now is to sit back, relax and enjoy the ride. And by the way, you might want to, "Fasten your seatbelt."

Prologue

*I*mmediately after takeoff, the chimes rang signaling the flight attendants to pick up the phone. The captain asked with urgency, "Do you smell anything in the cabin?" A tiny window on the exit door beamed in a ray of sunshine filled with dust particles glistening in the air. The dust began to churn and thicken like fog. Then it dawned on me: *That's not dust, that's smoke!* In disbelief, I peered into the coach section and my worst fear came true. A gray haze floated lightly throughout the cabin. I quickly relayed the information to the captain. We're turning around," he replied without hesitation. I said, "Terry, you grab the fire extinguishers and I'll find the source of the smoke..."

*O*n the morning of September 11, 2001, while stranded on the runway for three hours in Chicago, the captain informed us a gate was finally available, but he would have to call the chief of pilots to brief him on our situation. A few minutes later the phone chimed, "We are a security risk and can't come to the gate. They are going to storm the airplane from the rear. Disarm your doors in the back of the cabin…"

I knew I should have trusted my instincts by not going out with a stranger on a layover. A tear fell down my cheek as I looked into his eyes. They were glazed over with an animalistic look to them. I thought to myself, *I am either going to be raped or killed. No one knows where I am…*

As the hour grew close to midnight, the trapped passengers who were once calm and subdued lost all dignity by definition. Call lights chimed in frustration. The passengers began to chant. "WE WANT OFF, WE WANT OFF!" I called the captain to let him in on the action. "You might want to hear this…"

After a long grueling day, I couldn't wait to take a short break. Unfortunately, the unwanted sound of the phone chimed. Shelly, the first class flight attendant, yelled, "Get up here, NOW!" I made my way through coach wondering what I was going to find. As I entered first class, the putrid smell of vomit permeated the air. I continued to where the commotion was taking place in the first row. There, a man's body lay lifeless, slumped to the left. Fluids seeped from his mouth and his face was ashen. As I approached him, his eyes opened slightly. *Thank God he's alive.* I unlocked the oxygen from the bracket...

*W*hile filling my tank in uniform at the gas station, a young man opposite of me spoke up with curiosity, "You're a flight attendant, huh? I bet you have some stories to tell..."

1

A Dream Takes Flight

*O*ne summer Sunday afternoon my parents took all five of us children to the airport. My father parked the car on an old dirt road at the end of the runway to watch the airplanes take off and land. Barely 10 years old, I felt a surge of excitement as the engines revved up and the plane cruised toward us faster and faster. With a sudden burst and a roar, the aircraft soared above our heads. We watched in awe as it faded out of sight.

Each time we visited the airport, the excitement returned. One day, my parents took us inside the airport just for the fun of it. I observed the crewmembers as they passed by. The flight attendants looked so glamorous in their uniforms and high heels. They had a movie star air about them as they confidently strolled by us. *That is what I want to be when I grow up.*

In reality, our parents had just enough money to raise their five children, so flying on an airplane was a luxury we could not afford. My mother mentioned she would love to visit Europe someday. I assured her, "Don't worry Mom, one day I'll become a stewardess and you will get to go to Europe."

I kept that dream throughout high school and was determined to fly. I attended Barbizon Modeling School in St. Louis with the intention of pursuing my career. (Barbizon's famous slogan was "Be a model or just look like one.") Barely clearing 5' 4", I knew I could only look like one. In the early 80s, women were somewhat limited in their career choices. Most became nurses, some became teachers, and others enjoyed being a housewife. All I wanted to do was leave my small town in southern Illinois and experience life.

My initial airline interview took place in a neighboring state. The airline paid for my ticket to attend. As the airplane took off, I sat glued to the window in childlike wonder. Flying for the first time was everything I dreamed of and more.

On board, I watched the flight attendants serving beverages from the cart. After the service was completed, I noticed they were in the first class galley laughing and having a good old time. *This was the perfect job for me*! I opened my notebook and began reviewing questions I thought might be asked in the interview.

As the plane began its descent, I checked in the mirror for last minute touch-ups. While powdering my nose, I was pleased my long brown hair still had a little curl to it. I gazed down at my wine-colored suit and straightened out the wrinkles. *I love this pink ruffled shirt*, I mused, clueless of my unprofessional attire.

After deplaning, I entered the airline's office where a subdued gentleman escorted me to a room that felt more like an interrogation office. The moment I walked in I felt intimidated. A lady with her glasses sitting on the tip of her nose sat behind a desk staring at me critically. She was not exactly the warm and friendly type. She fired questions at me, none of which were on my list.

"Why did you choose to attend a Bible college?" she inquired.

I let out a nervous laugh and said, "Because my dad insisted."

There was no laughter from her. She continued her pointed barrage, "Are you prepared to relocate?"

"Where would I go?" I asked innocently. I knew when I walked out of that room this was not going to be my airline.

The very next day I had a group interview with another major airline. I smiled really big and raised my hand to answer all the questions being asked. At the end of the interview, the person asking the questions pulled me aside. "Next time," she said with a smile, "Put your hair up." I was devastated! If I had done that, you wouldn't have been able to see my curls!

After these setbacks, I waited two more years to apply for a position with another major airline.

2

The Final Interview

While reading the Sunday paper, I saw the ad in bold print: **Hiring Flight Attendants**. My mind raced. *Should I try again? What if I get rejected? Do I want to move somewhere else?* Deciding I had nothing to lose, I applied.

For weeks I eagerly checked the mailbox for the letter that would say, "You have been chosen for an interview with our airline." Finally the letter arrived. Excitedly, I ripped it open. The letter provided the details for the interview time and place. I looked up at the sky where I saw a jet flying. *Wow, that could be me up there someday.*

At the time, I lived in Atlanta and was working for a mortgage banking firm that offered upper level career opportunities for women. When I told my supervisor of my decision to interview for the flight attendant position, he cautioned, "Are you sure you want to give up what we have to offer? You know you could make a lot of money in the future." But I knew in my heart that this might be my last chance to pursue my dream.

I flew to the city where the interviews were being held. This time, I wore a very expensive navy-blue suit with a crisp, white shirt. My nails were perfect and, of course, my hair was tucked in a professional French twist. This time I had the vision. There was no doubt in my mind: *I was going to become a flight attendant.*

The applicants were asked to take a pencil and write a short essay on why they wanted to become flight attendants. Next, an attractive female interviewer ushered six of us into a room to ask a few questions. I made sure I was the first, second or third person to answer the questions as I did not want to have the same response as the other interviewees.

"What is your main weakness?" was the first question.

"Sometimes it is hard for me to say no to friends and family," I replied.

A girl sitting next to me who also wore a navy-blue suit was unfortunately too honest and said, "At times I feel unworthy and insecure." I instinctively knew it was over for her.

The interviewer then asked, "If you were sitting in first class, whom would you like to sit next to and why?" Others responded with names like President Reagan or Mahatma Gandhi.

I had a longer answer. "I watch a certain soap opera and one of the female characters is rumored to be a male in real life. I would love to sit next to her or him and get the scoop." They all laughed.

"Why do you want to become a flight attendant without using the words people or travel?"

Good question, I thought. "It fits my personality," I said. I felt confident about my responses to the six questions.

The interviewer thanked us for our time. As I was walking out the door, she pulled me to the side and asked, "Would you be able to go to the medical department and take your physical today?"

"Yes!" I jumped up and down with joy on the inside but continued to be poised and professional. *Wow, this is it, I am on my way!*

As I proceeded with my paperwork to another building, I passed by a pool with a large inflated raft floating on the water. It was the kind of raft one would see on an ocean occupied by survivors waiting to be rescued. Surrounding the pool were simulators of airplanes used during crew training. An inflated evacuation slide was attached to an opened airplane door. I began to feel nervous but continued walking to the medical department.

The first part of my exam was a hearing test. A female medical examiner led me into a tiny, windowless room. There, she put huge ear phones on my head. If I were to hear any beeps, I would raise my hand. I listened intently to loud then soft beeps. At times I heard a sound so faint I wasn't sure if it was even there, but I raised my hand anyway. Maybe this was just a stress test. If you were claustrophobic, you wouldn't last long in that room.

After passing a vision exam along with a weight check, I was told the tests were over. The airline would inform me by mail regarding their hiring decision. I flew home to Atlanta exhausted.

3

Charm Farm

And so began the vigil. After two long weeks of gut-wrenching anticipation, a large manila envelope with an airline logo on it arrived. I tore it open and read the letter out loud. "You have been accepted for flight attendant training." I screamed and ran into the house to share the good news with mom and dad and started packing my clothes for the next six weeks.

Little did I know those weeks would resemble boot camp. Fifty-two trainees attended our class: four of them would not make it to the end.

Along with the acceptance letter came three pages of airport codes. In two weeks, training would begin and all codes had to be memorized before we arrived. Those starting with the first three letters of a city — ATL for Atlanta, MIA for Miami — were easy to remember. Others like ORD for Chicago, MSY for New Orleans and SNA for Orange County were more difficult.

My first day of training wasn't too bad. Each of the students had to stand in front of the classroom and tell a few informative facts about themselves. At the end of the day we piled into a van that took us to our home away from home: a nice enough hotel. Each of us shared a room with another trainee. It was a little scary to have a complete stranger as a roommate, but I was lucky to have one I liked. It was one of many adjustments to come.

During the job interview we were asked, "If you had to move to a new location, would you do it?"

"Yes," We all agreed.

"If you were asked to cut your hair, would you do it?"

"Yes." Again we all agreed in unison.

Now the time had come. Every Monday we had to pass a grooming and weight check. On the second Monday, the instructor asked, "Are you prepared to cut your hair?" Of course I said, "Yes," but dreaded it. It took years to grow my hair down to my waist and it was cut off with one whack! My new look was now a perfect bob (chin length hair) that mirrored everyone else's.

Some of the girls would starve themselves over the weekend in order to not exceed their weight limit. Our weight had to match our height's profile. If we were 1 pound over, we were let go. In my 20s I was thin, so the weight checks were not an issue for me. However, I felt sorry for those who struggled with those weight restrictions.

Nights were consumed with studying. I wanted this job more than anything in the world. In the fourth week of training we attended a workshop on oxygen use. The instructor asked, "If you screwed the lid on the oxygen unit, would you turn it tightly or finger-tight?" I panicked, not knowing the answer. Common sense said tightly, but I was wrong. I'd received A's on all my tests so far. Now, because of this incorrect answer, I felt something changed in the relationship between the instructor and me. I saw the look of uncertainty on her face and now felt like I was being observed warily for the first time. It was unnerving because several students had disappeared throughout training. None of us received any explanations as to where or why they had gone. Apparently, the instructors simply decided they weren't flight attendant material.

I was sitting in the classroom when a female instructor entered. "Miss Churchill," she said sternly, "You need to come with me." *Oh no, not me.*

I waited for an hour or so outside the instructor's office. Apparently she forgot I was there because when she saw me she simply said, "Oh, I just wanted to let you know you need to put more blush on your cheeks." Not wanting to make any issues I simply replied, "No problem." Flight attendant grooming required that our lips had to be seen from across the room and our nails needed to match our lip color. The preferred color was bright red.

Anytime an instructor approached us, my group of friends and I laughed with each other pretending we were in an engaging conversation. The fact is we were stressed beyond description and exhausted from the amount of information being pumped into our heads.

We were taught how to deal with a variety of medical emergencies. This included epileptic seizures, bloody noses, upset stomachs, diabetic attacks, broken bones, fainting spells, and even death. When it came time to view the childbirth video, many of the students (especially the male trainees) turned their heads. They could handle emergencies like a heart attack or death, but not a video on childbirth. Go figure.

Halon or H2O extinguishers are used to fight the three classes of fire. We needed to know which type most effectively puts out each class of fire. For example, if it were a Class A or material fire, we would use the H2O extinguisher. A Class C or electrical fire required the Halon. To extinguish a fire, we must aim at the base of the fire, not at the flames. Our test was to gather around the fire pit and put out a fire. The flight attendants lined up in a mock demonstration and took turns practicing the use of the extinguishers.

On each flight, the flight attendants have an assigned, numbered position. This number dictates which cabin to work and what responsibilities we will have. The number one flight attendant always works first class and has the most interaction with the pilots. The number two position is in charge of the main cabin galley on all aircrafts. If it is a larger aircraft, more flight attendant positions are needed.

During our training, the aircrafts included the narrow-body 727-100, 727-200 and MD-9, (Super-80) and the wide-body A-300 airbus, DC-10, 757 and 767. We were required to memorize where the emergency equipment was located, how to open each exit door, and the commands for the different doors for each aircraft. A single door exit means passengers can evacuate one at a time. Dual doors allow two passengers to deplane simultaneously. Window exits can be used for passengers to walk out on the wing to escape. Some have slides attached to them, and some do not.

The evacuation command is specific for each type of aircraft and exit. At the end of the six week period, we must say the commands and open the windows and doors in front of the instructors. We refer these tasks as drills. Up to three attempts were allowed to successfully complete the drills on day one. If we did not say them perfectly after the third attempt, we had one last, desperate try remaining, which was scheduled for the next day. Failure to achieve perfection resulted in termination.

I was exhausted!

With anticipation and trepidation, the moment of truth had arrived. It was time for our examination (drills). The trainees timidly walked into the training area filled with the simulator airplanes. I am a believer in going first and getting things out of the way, so I volunteered to do the commands for the window exit first. "Don't take anything with you," I shouted. "You stay on the wing, help the people out, send them that way." "Step through, foot first." The instructor took my paperwork and wrote that I did an outstanding job. *Whew!* On to the next aircraft.

When I initially took my medical exam, I noticed one of the slides on a simulator door deployed. Now I found out what it was used for; we had to jump onto the slide as if we were in a real evacuation. Somehow this slide was more intimidating than the slides we played on when we were children. The instructors gave us jumpsuits and footies to wear so we wouldn't get hurt. It was my turn next. Knowing I was still being evaluated, I pretended to be brave and stood at the top of the exit.

I smiled at the instructor as she nodded for me to jump. My hands stretched out as instructed and I took a big leap. As I was going down the slide, my footie slipped off my heel. I felt a burning sensation and pain but didn't say a word. After reaching the bottom of the slide, I took off the sock. Skin mixed with blood was dangling off my ankle. I still didn't say a word.

The hard part was over. I passed the examination and finally the day we dreamed of arrived. Graduation! We joyfully sang our class song, and I was so happy. I did it! I was now officially a flight attendant for a major airline.

It has been more than 25 years since then, and from what I understand "the charm farm" has become less rigid. Looking back, I realize the instructors needed to toughen us up and see what we were made of. I'm just glad I survived. I am also grateful for the rigorous training which prepared me for the many crisis situations that lay ahead.

The unrealistic weight requirements have long been relaxed and as long as flight attendants can fit through an airplane window exit and put a seat belt on without an extension, they can fly.

4

First Lesson

$\mathcal{D}$uring training, one of the instructors jokingly said, "Now girls, you stay away from those pilots!" That remark was long forgotten by the time I took off on my first official working flight.

We were flying from Dallas/Ft. Worth to Orlando. I couldn't wait to go. Stepping on the Super-80 aircraft was like walking on the moon to me. After introducing myself to the three flight attendants working the cabin, I poked my head into the cockpit.

"Hi, I'm Chris, your number four flight attendant."

The captain was in his late 50s with gray hair and deep wrinkles. "Hi, I'm Joe and this is First Officer Rick."

"It's nice to meet you," I said. I glanced at them and noticed how handsome they looked in their uniforms. *Wow, real pilots.*

The gate agent came on the aircraft notifying us it was time to board. I felt a little nervous and awkward standing in front of the forward entry door. As the passengers boarded, I welcomed them. "Good morning," "Hello," "How are you?" The nervousness gradually diminished and excitement took its place.

After takeoff, my fellow coach flight attendant, Jessica, and I served a delicious breakfast with a choice of pancakes or cheddar cheese omelets. *This is the greatest job ever,* I thought to myself, while eating a leftover omelet in the galley. Later, I went through the cabin offering pillows, blankets and magazines.

As the aircraft began its descent, I anticipated all the fun things we could do on our long layover in Orlando. "Flight attendants, prepare for landing," the captain announced.

We arrived in Orlando around 11:30 a.m., and I was ready to go out and see the sights. However, none of the flight attendants cared to do anything. But the captain did, and asked if I would like to get an ice cream cone with him. That sounded like a good idea to me. After all, it was my very first trip.

Captain Joe and I walked across the street and tasted the best orange sherbet I had ever eaten. We slurped our ice cream cones and headed back to the hotel.

"Hey, would you like to see some pictures of my boat?" he asked.

"Sure," I said, not wanting to be rude.

We walked into the room and sat on the edge of the bed looking at his pictures. Suddenly I felt his fingers creeping around my neck. I was appalled. Being in my early 20s, this guy could be my grandfather. I jumped up, made some kind of excuse, and got the heck out of there.

"*Stay away from those pilots,*" *hmm*! Yep, lesson learned; but soon forgotten!

5

Dallas versus New York

As newly hired flight attendants, we had the opportunity to choose the base of our choice. The instructors called it our wish list. Two bases were opened for our class, New York or Dallas. My first choice was Dallas and luckily I held it.

In training, we heard there was some sort of rivalry between the Dallas based and the New York based flight attendants. In fact, there was a phrase quoted by New York flight attendants, "Death before Dallas."

I was put on reserve right away. Being on reserve meant we were on call and never knew when or where our next trip was going to take us. For most of my trips, I was called out for what was referred to as an extra position. Basically, that means we are covering a very full flight where extra help is required. During each trip flown, I pretended like I knew what I was doing and had flown all my life. At the end of the flight,

I informed the flight attendants that I was brand new. I soaked up all the praise they gave me.

My second month of flying, I wasn't so lucky. I received the call for a DC-10 flight. This was one of our largest aircraft we had at the time. I walked on the airplane and again was going to pretend like I knew what I was doing even though I had never stepped foot on a DC-10.

As I walked on the airplane, my confidence immediately was shattered. All of the flight attendants were senior (a.k.a. skynosaurs). What was scarier, they were all New York based.

They were cackling in the galley as I entered. The conversation stopped as their eyes shifted toward me. *Please don't ask me where I am based.* Unfortunately, the first question asked by one of the flight attendants was just that. I told them proudly, and they shrieked and giggled like witches brewing up a scheme for their next victim. I felt uneasy and quickly evacuated the galley.

The whole flight was a nightmare. I heard one of the flight attendants ask, "Where is she, where is she?" I tried to hide from her, but when the old biddy found me she threw an empty insert at me. "Go pick up the cabin," she commanded. They all bossed me around until I locked myself into the lavatory. That happened only once, but it was devastating.

The rivalry between the bases has long been forgotten, but the memory of that day still lingers.

6

Probation

*W*hen training was over, we thought we were home free. But in reality an eight month probation period was still ahead. We couldn't call in sick, have a late sign-in for our trip, and we certainly didn't want any bad letters from passengers.

After a couple of months of flying, I started to get the hang of it. I just loved it. It was everything I imagined and more. The passengers were always nice to me and appreciated my smiles. I received many thank you cards and letters of commendation.

One morning, I was called out for a reserve trip to fly first class on a DC-10. The entire crew was brand new. As we boarded the flight, I noticed a passenger plunking himself down in my section in first class. He certainly had not cleaned up for the flight and was wearing a navy blue uniform with an embroidered name-tag on it. His hair looked like Albert Einstein's and he had a salt and pepper untrimmed gray mustache. His

demeanor was overbearing and he obviously loved the attention (albeit negative) the passengers were giving him.

On some flights we serve only orange juice or champagne
for our pre-departure beverage service. This was one of those
flights. I stopped at the obnoxious guy and asked which one he
preferred.

"I want a beer," he demanded. He poured on the charm and
showered me with compliments.

I said, "I'm sorry, but the beverages are down in the lower
galley of the airplane. "OJ or champagne?"

He took my hand and said, "Come `ere." To my horror, he
forced my lips to his. Then, he laughed hysterically. His breath
reeked of alcohol, so I knew he had been drinking prior to the
flight. "Now go get me some G__ D___ beer," he commanded.
Totally disgusted, I ran to the restroom to wash my lips, and
then I rushed to the galley flight attendant. "I think we have a
problem here. No, I KNOW we have a problem."

I continued hanging the passengers' jackets as they boarded the aircraft. "EXCUSE ME," I heard in the distance from
the Jerk.

Cautiously approaching him, I said, "How can I help you?"

He acted as though he was going to whisper something in
my ear, but he grabbed and pushed my head down to his crotch.
Mortified, I wanted to take my lovely silver serving tray and

bash him over the head. Several passengers in first class saw the incident, but no one knew what to do.

The gate agent boarded the aircraft. "Well, I've got some bad news for you. We are delayed by an hour for takeoff because of aircraft traffic holds into Chicago." *Oh great, that is all I need.* I told her about the unbelievably crude passenger and asked if she could remove him from the flight. She said she would check his itinerary and be back in a few minutes.

Meanwhile, the passenger acted as though he had done nothing wrong and was again trying to charm me. The galley flight attendant suggested I go ahead and give him his beer to shut him up. *I hate rewarding bad behavior.*

I rushed into the cockpit to complain about this guy.

"We really need to get this passenger off," I said.

The pilots were junior also. The captain said, "Well, uh, I'd appreciate it if you could handle it back there, but if you can't, let me know."

The agent returned to the aircraft. "I am really sorry you guys," she said. "The passenger has 425,000 miles in our mileage program." At the time, the program was fairly new, so 425,000 was a big deal. "I can't take him off the aircraft, but I will personally talk to him." *I couldn't believe it.*

The first class flight attendants and I huddled around to watch as she had her little chat with the passenger. At least he did not do what he had done to me, but we could see his temper flaring. The agent came to us white as a ghost. "I told him he couldn't have anything to drink for the rest of the flight." she said as she turned around and walked off the aircraft. *Oh great!*

I walked past the misbehaving passenger to pick up some glasses from our pre-departure service. On the way back, he once again stopped me. The sweetness in his voice was now bitter. "No one has ever challenged me on the aircraft. Do you know how much I fly? I am going to have your job." I just looked at him and smiled politely. Still having several months of probation left to go, I wasn't going to let this idiot ruin my career.

An hour passed and as promised the airplane taxied away from the gate. This was a quick dinner flight from Dallas to Chicago. The flight attendants had to work hard to accomplish the service. As I passed by Mr. Obnoxious, he stuck his leg out and tried to trip me. Later, I heard his calling whistle. I worked the other aisle in an attempt to avoid him. Nevertheless, I still heard his outrageous remarks. "Hey b----, get over here, use this aisle." I had never been treated this way in my life. The other passengers must have been afraid of him because no one intervened.

Finally, the dinner service was over and we landed. I did it!

Today, twenty some years later, I could have that passenger arrested for crew interference and assault. The flight attendants and agents are not allowed to board any intoxicated passenger.

7

Decompression

A long time ago, we had a fleet of 727 aircraft. The airplanes aged and were no longer cost effective, so our airline fazed them out. We were working a flight from Toronto to New York. It's a very short flight, but somehow our 727 managed to give us a headache, or on this flight, an earache.

After the plane took off, it was ascending its way to 33,000 feet. It didn't quite make it, though. My ears began to hurt. They plugged up and wouldn't clear. I did the Valsalva maneuver (pinch your nose, close your mouth and gently try to blow air through your nose). I tried to yawn really big and kept swallowing, hoping to clear my ears. It wasn't working.

Looking into the cabin, I saw some of the passengers holding their ears with their mouths wide open. It actually looked comical, but under the circumstances wasn't funny at all.

I was the number one flight attendant. Our procedure for an emergency situation is to go to the cockpit and ask the captain for pertinent information: How much time do we have? Are we going to evacuate? What's the signal for an evacuation?

I entered the cockpit and saw all three pilots with their oxygen masks on. *This can't be good.* I heard the flight engineer say, "It's going out, it's going out, there goes the automatic, and there goes the manual." Apparently, a tear in the pressurization seal had occurred. I felt my body tense and stood for a moment in shock. When the pilots noticed me, they waved me out of the cockpit. *What about my information?* I left the cockpit with my ears still hurting.

Now knowing we were in an emergency situation, I scrambled to the galley to lock it up. The aircraft took an immediate dive. I grabbed the oven door to catch my balance. Within seconds the plane leveled out and reached a safe cruising altitude below 10,000 feet. If they had continued to fly the plane at the higher altitude, the passengers would have had up to three minutes without oxygen before they lost consciousness. The ear pain eased, and due to the close proximity of New York, we continued on with the flight without further incident.

Later, the captain said because we had not reached our cruising altitude, he made the decision not to deploy the oxygen masks. Now, all of our aircrafts have an automatic deployment system.

There are three types of decompression: slow, rapid and explosive. On this flight, we had a slow decompression.

A rapid decompression could include cheek and lip flutter along with ear pain and the possibility of chest expansion. This can occur due to a malfunction of the pressurization system.

An explosive decompression can occur quickly due to a tear or hole in the fuselage (the aircraft's body). This could cause a loud bang or rushing air. There may be flying debris along with fog in the cabin. A decrease in temperature may also occur. At this time the oxygen masks immediately drop. Passengers using oxygen would do so until the captain says it is safe to breathe on your own.

A decompression is a very rare occurrence.

8

The Mile High Club

$\mathcal{D}$on't ask me why anyone would want to have sexual escapades in the airplane lavatory. But it happens all the time. Well, actually I only saw it happen two times, but I hear about it frequently.

I was asked, "Have you ever joined the mile-high club?" What is that? I asked naively. *We fly a lot higher than a mile.* When I found out what it was, I was pretty disgusted. If anyone knew how much urine or vomit was on the restroom floor, I guarantee the romance would fizzle in a flash.

I was working a trip with a friend of mine. We commented at the beginning of the flight how cute and in love this one couple looked. It was a night flight, so the cabin was romantically dim.

I was in the first class galley when my friend Stephanie called.

"Hey, I'm on the back jumpseat. The male passenger went into the lavatory. He was in there for a minute or two when his partner came to join him."

"I'll be right there," I excitedly said.

Thank goodness we didn't have any passengers who needed to use the restroom because they were in there for more than just a quickie. Stephanie and I had our ears glued to the door and tried to contain our laughter. When we heard the door unlock, we fled the scene.

The other time was not so funny. I was welcoming the passengers on board, when I, along with everyone else, noticed a female who was scantily dressed. She wore a very short, black patent-leather skirt with a zipper on the back and looked like a prostitute. She pranced to the back of the aircraft — all eyeballs following her.

A handsome businessman was behind her while boarding. He sat next to her, but it didn't seem like they belonged together. Sure enough, my instincts were right. I stopped to chat with them. He chuckled while speaking, "Yeah, we met out in the airport bar. She said she'd give me $10 if I would sit next to her on the flight." *Hmmm, I see a ring on his finger.*

They purchased a few more drinks on the flight. I walked by and saw him giving his new friend a back rub. *Uh-oh.*

The next time I walked by, tongues were flashing between passionate kisses. *This was not good.*

Then, neither one were in their row of seats. I went to the back where the lavatories were located. Only one of the two was occupied. I waited by the door feeling as though I were taking on the role of a very disapproving chaperone.

Click went the door and out she pranced. She smirked at me, fluffed her hair, and walked on by. The door opened again and out came the businessman. He looked at me with a grin bigger than the Grinch's. *Shame on you.*

After landing and deplaning, I walked behind them. The man's wife and three children were there to meet him. He gave his wife a quick peck on the lips and hugged the kids. His in-flight companion's boyfriend was there to meet her. They walked off hand-in-hand.

9

He Asked for It!

*O*ne of my friends and I used to fly together all the time. We loved our jobs and tried to help out people as much as possible. On this flight we were flying to an international destination, so you have to clear Customs and Immigration after landing.

After everyone deplaned, an older gentleman remained sitting in first class. "Where's my wheelchair?" he demanded. Usually, the gate agent is right there to meet the flight. A passenger service assistant is responsible for all wheelchairs. On this particular flight, there was no one around.

We waited and waited. The older passenger became more and more furious. I didn't blame him. We couldn't look for an agent because the crew also had to clear customs. A wheelchair on the jet bridge was available, just no one to push it.

At this point, the old man was losing it. "Get me off this !#%! airplane, *NOW!*"

Flight attendants are not responsible for providing wheelchair assistance, possibly because of what was about to happen.

My friend said if I pulled her luggage, she'd push the wheelchair. I agreed. She struggled to push it up the jet bridge. Not too far down the hallway we approached a long, moving sidewalk. She instinctively walked on with the wheelchair. A wheel got stuck on the silver bar attached to the sidewalk, and the wheelchair lifted from the back spilling the old guy out. He cruised down the moving sidewalk with his arms and legs flailing while screaming obscenities that I won't mention.

The situation though serious, also struck us as absolutely hilarious! We turned around and laughed so hard I almost wet my pants.

After gaining our composure, we raced down to the other end of the moving sidewalk and helped the man back into his wheelchair. He wasn't hurt physically, but he had a few more choice words to say to us, despite our profuse apologies.

I bet the next time he won't be so demanding.

10

Another Missing Statistic

After three years of flying out of Dallas, Raleigh/Durham opened as a crew base. I put my transfer in and was accepted. It was a small base so everyone knew each other. The pilots, flight attendants and agents were one big family.

I grew up mainly in the Midwest, so I guess you could say I was a little naïve. I experienced the normal growing up relationships with a few boyfriends along the way. I trusted everyone, including strangers. I came to realize not everyone can be trusted and was about to learn just how dangerous life could be.

My trip laid over in sunny West Palm Beach, Florida. Our flight arrived around noon, which meant we practically had the whole day to play. With the mall down the street from the hotel, I decided to do some shopping.

I moseyed into an interior design shop. A good looking man with dark hair and a warm smile approached me. I am not sure what his opening line was, but I fell for it. During the conversation, he asked my name and where I was staying. I certainly didn't think I was giving him information; I thought we were just talking.

After about thirty minutes, he said, "Nice to meet you", and went on his way. *I was shocked! I wondered why he didn't ask for my number. Oh well!*

I finished my shopping and went back to the hotel. Later that evening around 5 p.m., the phone rang. It was him! He exclaimed how beautiful the city was at night and how he would love to show me around in his convertible. I told him it's not that I didn't trust him; I couldn't go out because I was on a layover.

I gave him my home phone number in Raleigh. His brother also lived in North Carolina, so we had some connections and things in common. He said okay and hung up the telephone.

My thoughts began to race. *Shoot! Here I am sitting in the hotel doing absolutely nothing, I should have gone.* Around 6 p.m., the phone rang again. "Come on Chris, it's absolutely gorgeous outside, not a cloud in the sky."

My instincts said no, but the adventurer in me won over. "Okay, I'll go."

He pulled up to the hotel in a black Mercedes convertible. *Wow!*

The first thing he said was, "I forgot my wallet. Would you mind if I stop by my house to get it?"

My guard went up a bit but I said, "Not at all."

He took me to a beautiful gated community. His house was tucked away in the corner of a cul-de-sac surrounded by a pristine lake. It was gorgeous!

"Come on in, I'll give you a tour, I even designed my own pillows."

I certainly didn't think anything was wrong with going in, so I followed him. He gave me the full tour.

We sat down on the couch together.

He said, "You know, I don't drink, I don't smoke, and if it wasn't for God, I wouldn't have any of these things."

Wow! He's handsome, good morals and values, and he obviously has money. This guy is too good to be true.

We sat talking about mundane things...flying, the weather...there was nothing to prepare me for what happened next. He fixed his eyes on me with a predatory gaze and lunged toward me. His kisses turned to chewing and slobbering. My cheeks, my forehead and my chin were now covered with his foul smelling saliva. His hands were everywhere as he spouted language straight out of a hard core porn magazine. "The breasts over in Europe are free for all to see," he muttered.

Terrified, I glanced in his eyes. They seemed glazed with an animalistic look. He clearly was not there. I told him the crew was meeting around 9 o'clock, and I need to get back to the hotel. It didn't faze him. He continued groping and spewing his filth. I knew I was in serious trouble.

I am either going to be raped or killed. I may be one of those missing statistics. No one knows where I am.

I thought maybe I should slap him and call a cab, but didn't want to anger him…he was out of control. Even if I could reach a phone, I had no idea where I was located.

By this time, tears streamed down my face. It still did not faze him. While he was slobbering all over me, he had somehow unzipped his pants. He tried to put my hand on his hardened penis, but I kept pulling it away.

He started playing with himself and then came all over his stomach. Slowly he regained his composure and his glazed eyes focused on me. My gut instinct told me to play it cool.

I said, "Hey listen, I really need to get back to the hotel."

He started to freak out. "I don't want this to be just a one night stand, and I really want to see you again." he ranted.

I replied with a calm demeanor, "Don't worry about it… it's no big deal."

It was the biggest lie I had ever told, but he seemed pacified. He took me to the hotel. On our way there he said, "I want to walk you to your room so that you will be safe." I couldn't believe it. *Safe, safe?*

As soon as we were close to the hotel, and the car slowed to a stop, I jumped out and ran straight to my room making sure the dead bolt was locked. I took a hot shower to calm myself and wash his foulness away.

I didn't hear from him again, thank God.

Many people ask why I didn't call the police. I'm not sure. Maybe, it was because I felt ashamed I had been so naïve and I didn't even know his name or where he lived. I was traumatized and all I wanted to do was forget what happened. It was another valuable lesson learned.

11

Sparks Everywhere

$\mathscr{R}$aleigh crew base was just like a small town. I knew I had to be very careful. Everyone knew each other's business.

I was the number one flight attendant working from Raleigh to Chicago. When the cockpit crew entered the aircraft, I immediately felt an attraction for the first officer, Kirk. In our small town, I had heard of him and also knew he had a girlfriend.

We were on a 727 aircraft with three pilots in the cockpit. Knowing Kirk was involved with someone else, I avoided him as much as possible. It was difficult because I not only served first class but also provided meal service to the cockpit crew. Just being near him flustered me and I kept forgetting their meal orders. It's amazing what chemistry can do.

We landed in Chicago. Our schedule was to continue on to St. Louis to rest for the night. After all passengers were boarded, our aircraft heading for St. Louis pushed away from the gate. While doing so, an indicator light lit up in the cockpit

forcing us to the return to the jet bridge. When a light illumi-
nates, it means one of two things: a mechanical issue or a light
malfunction. The mechanics said in this case it was simply the
light, so we pushed away from the gate again.

Taxiing along the tarmac, the captain noticed a tiny crack
in the cockpit window.

This time we were in for a lengthy delay.

I tried to stay away from First Officer Kirk as much as possible, but due to the mechanical issue, I had to interact to keep
the communication going between the pilots, flight attendants
and passengers. Finally, the captain made a judgment call not
to continue on with the damaged aircraft, which resulted in a
cancellation of the flight.

The crewmembers piled into the van that took us to our
hotel. Kirk sat next to me, but we never spoke. He accidentally
brushed against me while the driver took a severe turn. I felt
a tingle where he touched me. He smiled and apologized. I
looked down bashfully.

The next morning our pickup was bright and early. We were
supposed to work one flight home to Raleigh and that was it.
After arriving at the airport, we were informed by our scheduling department that a reassignment had been given to us and
would now be working a flight from Dallas with a layover in

Birmingham. The best part about our job is going home, so naturally we were a little disappointed.

I once again stayed away from Kirk. I could tell he was a little nervous around me too.

The van pulled into the hotel's circular driveway in Birmingham. After registering, the crew strolled to the elevator. The first officer and I were behind the rest of them. The elevator was already packed, so Kirk told the crew to go ahead. The two of us stood in silence for another door to open.

After the elevator door closed, he looked me straight in the eye and said, "Now listen, I am supposed to be getting married and we already have our invitations sent out. I have these feelings for you that I don't know what I am supposed to do with."

I was stunned and speechless. I felt like the movie *It's A Wonderful Life*, where George Bailey was yelling at Mary, then kissed her passionately. Only I didn't get the kiss.

I told him I was avoiding him because I knew he had a girlfriend. Nothing more was said. I proceeded to my room only to find him coming in my direction. He stopped when I stopped. *Oh no, not adjoining rooms.* This very seldom happens. I closed my door and looked at his connecting door slowly putting my hand on it. I felt as if he might have done the same.

I awakened the next morning to answer the ringing phone, hoping that it wasn't the scheduling department reassigning us again.

"Hello?" It was Kirk.

"Can we have breakfast together? I need to talk to you."

Our pick-up was at 2:15 p.m., so we had plenty of time.

While sipping our coffee, he said he had been thinking about me the whole night. Not wanting to make any mistakes, he didn't know what to do. We didn't really come to any conclusions, but trying to do what's right, we reluctantly returned to our rooms. Heart still pounding, I started packing my suitcase for our trip home to Raleigh.

While putting on my makeup, I noticed a peculiar smell in the air — it smelled like smoke. Soon, fire engines roared to the front of our hotel. I ran to the window in disbelief. I looked for possible escape routes and noticed I was way too high to jump. I ran to the door and felt it with the back of my hand to make sure it wasn't hot.

It's amazing how our training always kicks in when emergencies arise. It wasn't hot, so I opened the door. Smoke was everywhere! The alarm was not sounding, and no one was in the hall. My first thought was everyone had forgotten about me. I knocked on Kirk's door, but he didn't answer. It was one o'clock in the afternoon, so it wasn't unusual not to have guests at that time. *But where was my crew?* I heard a click down the hall and the flight engineers' door opened.

"What's going on?" He yelled. "I smell smoke."

"Me too," I shouted back, "We're on fire!"

We ran to the elevator, but it wasn't operating. While sprinting in the other direction toward the stairs, the captain stuck his head out of his room.

"Hey, I just talked to the front desk. There is a fire on the twelfth floor." (We were on the tenth.) "Don't worry about getting your things; I will meet you downstairs."

The captain was married to one of the flight attendants, so I knew she would be okay. The other flight attendant poked her soaking wet head out the door. She had only her bra and underwear on, so she quickly threw on some clothes and down the stairs we went.

About 45 minutes had gone by. The firefighters said the fire was under control, but the elevators would remain closed. We knew what that meant: more stairs! I was not looking forward to walking up ten flights, getting dressed, and then carrying my bags back down.

When I finally reached my room, I knocked on Kirk's door again. He had been in the shower when I knocked the first time. I mistakenly thought he must have gone downstairs when he didn't answer. He said he smelled the smoke, but figured if the alarms weren't going off it must not have been anything to worry about. I never did find out why the alarms weren't sounding.

I carried my bags down the winding staircase which still had a hint of smoke filtering in. Round and round I went, having to stop now and then because the bags felt more like bricks than luggage. Finally, I reached the bottom of the ten floors. The driver took my bags from me as the crew gathered in the van. Surprisingly enough, we made it on time for our 2:15 pickup.

I was day dreaming out the window and noticed the sky was looking scary. A line of dark clouds hovered above the ground. Just at that moment, we heard the civil defense siren blaring. The alarmed van driver turned on the radio. A tornado warning was in effect for this county. We couldn't believe it! The van driver raced to the airport checking out the sky making sure there weren't any funnel clouds about to touch down in our path. When we arrived at the airport, the agents ushered us to a safe location. Thank God it never touched down.

Needless to say, the flight to Raleigh was cancelled. We sat around for a couple more hours, and then deadheaded on the next flight to Raleigh. (Deadhead means we travel just like a passenger but still get paid for it.) The agent handed us our boarding pass. I looked at mine and then the first officer's. How did I guess we would be sitting next to each other?

For the next couple of hours we laughed at how many things had happened to us. He lived right across the lake from me in Raleigh. We mutually agreed it was best to leave things the way they were. I see him from time to time. He married his girlfriend and has two beautiful children.

12

A-300 Scarebus

*O*ur trip looked harmless enough: Miami to San Jose, Costa Rica, and then return to Miami the next day.

The A-300 is one of our largest aircrafts, which holds up to 267 passengers. On this particular flight we were completely full. The flight attendants had a briefing with the pilots before the plane took off. "Well, the flight plan looks smooth on the way to Costa Rica, but there might be some weather when we arrive," the captain said. "I'll keep you advised." He didn't seem too concerned.

The flight was uneventful until we approached San Jose. Costa Rica is a breathtaking place to visit. The island has gorgeous waterfalls, lush greenery and mountains — mountains everywhere, including around the airport.

The captain called the flight attendants, "There are severe storms in the area. We will be circling in a holding pattern until it lifts. I will keep you posted." Looking at my watch, I knew we were not going to make our scheduled arrival time of 5 p.m. About an hour passed when the captain called again. "There is a passageway through the clouds that looks as though I can make an attempt to land." His voice was heard over the PA, "Prepare for landing!"

If we were in the States, we could divert to the closest city in an emergency or unfavorable weather conditions, but Costa Rica has only one major airport.

I sat down on my jumpseat in the back of the airplane along with Michael, the aft galley flight attendant. We gazed at each other in disbelief as the plane fought its way through the clouds. I felt my hands perspiring as I clung to the seat.

The sound of the landing gear was an indescribable relief, but as our airplane approached the runway, the engines suddenly revved up. The force of the ascent shoved us back into our seats and upward toward those unfriendly skies.

There was dead silence in the cabin. The captain had earlier informed the crew we were running low on fuel. I said to Michael in a low voice, "Do you know how much fuel it takes to take off like that?" The captain's voice returned on the PA. "Well, ahhh, ladies and gentlemen, ahhh, our cockpit instruments are not matching up to the runway. We're going to go around and try it again manually." *Oh great! We are maneuvering around the mountains, the daylight is now gone, and we are low on fuel.* The plane circled around, yet again. Every second felt like an eternity. We were still on our jumpseats when we heard the sound of the landing gear lowered again. I looked out the window and could see the lights below. I held my breath. *Lower, lower, lower.* Instead of feeling the landing gear touch the ground, the engines increased power. We shot up like a rocket being launched. The roar was unbelievable. Ding! Ding! It was the captain calling us. "You guys, we can't make it the third time. Our alternate is Panama City." The tightness in his voice was evident.

The crew gathered in the galley. We were all white as ghosts yet had to maintain our professionalism. I said, "I think we should say some prayers." At this point I felt out of control and needed some reassurance, so I went into the cockpit. That was a huge mistake. Some things are better off not knowing.

I quietly slid on the jumpseat behind the captain and desperately wanted them to tell me everything was going to be all right. The silence was deafening. I couldn't believe this was happening. The control tower from Panama City called. The message heard was relayed in English with a strong Spanish accent. "Due to the weather conditions, we are below minimums here; you can't land. Your alternate is Managua, Nicaragua."

My heart began to beat so hard I could feel it in my head. I noticed the captain had sweat beads forming on his forehead. He turned the airplane in the opposite direction, now heading for Managua.

"What are you doing?" I hear another voice in broken English. "You cannot land here. We are not equipped for your aircraft." The captain is now brushing sweat off his forehead with the back of his hand. "If you don't let us land this airplane, there is going to be a bird falling out of the sky," the captain said. Managua gave us the clearance.

At that point, I left the cockpit numb. The rest of the crew was waiting to hear some news. Unfortunately, there was no good news. The passengers realized something was terribly wrong. They sat in their seats in silence. I passed by them with a pleasant smile, but inside I was terrified. A lady stopped me. "I want to take a video of you. This is for our loved ones." I wanted to burst into tears and hug her; instead, I just smiled and waved into her camera. I walked away with a horrid vision of my mom and dad watching me in this video of my final moments on Earth or rather in the atmosphere.

We waited to hear from the pilots for what seemed like an eternity. *Were we going to run out of fuel at any moment? Were we going to be a big bird falling out of the sky?* The captain announced over the PA the words we had heard two times before on this flight, "Flight attendants, prepare for landing." The crew did the mandatory compliance check to make sure all the seatbacks were upright and all tray tables were stowed. My hands were tingling and my heart was in my throat. Michael and I returned to our jumpseats.

Every once in a while we glanced at each other in fear. Again, the landing gear lowered. I heard the familiar sound of it locking into place. *Please, please, God,* I pleaded. *Let us land safely.* Hours had now passed and exhaustion set in. My commands for opening my exit in an emergency went through my mind. The rain beat against the fuselage and the wind tore at the plane. As we struggled to land, the nose of the aircraft started to lift, but this time lowered itself onto the runway instead of rising to the sky. Thud! We made it. Everyone cheered, clapping uncontrollably.

We waited on the tarmac for a long time. My heart sank as I peered out the window and realized the incident was far from over. Outside, men with machine guns surrounded the airplane. Most people wanted to get off and check into a hotel. We couldn't because of all the regulations associated with Customs. Moreover, the political climate in Nicaragua at the time made it unsafe for Americans to be there.

When the control tower at Managua communicated the airport wasn't equipped for large aircrafts such as the A-300, they really meant it. They didn't have any way of reaching our fuel tanks to refill them. The only way they could think of was to use a ladder, but they didn't have one at the airport. A kind soul generously volunteered to drive to his nearby house to pick up his ladder.

The flight attendants provided a quick water service, pretending to be calm. Afterward, I sat on my jumpseat exhausted. My body started to tremble. *Oh my Gosh, I am going into shock. My body is going into shock and I am smiling and calming passengers. This is crazy!*

Hours passed, but we finally got refueled. The thought of heading back to Costa Rica didn't appeal to me, but the thought of being in a nice comfortable bed did. "Let's go," the captain said, "We have plenty of fuel this time and the weather is good." The aircraft taxied down the runway. "Flight attendants, prepare for departure." Michael and I exchanged eye contact with eyebrows lifted. It's amazing how you can tell what someone else is feeling without uttering a word.

We strapped into our jumpseats for the flight back to San Jose. Thank God our ice and supplies were depleted, so we did not have to do another service. Once again, the captain spoke humbly. "Flight attendants, prepare for landing." The landing gear lowered and again we waited. I said a quick prayer. Thud! We made it. The applause was thunderous. If the passengers had been allowed to get up, there would have been a standing ovation. What a trip!

I didn't fly to San Jose much after that. A week later, someone asked if I had heard about the A-300 that almost went down. "Yep, I responded, and I can tell you all about it."

13

Goodbye Forever, Chris

I never thought I would marry a sociopath, but I did. I never thought suicide would ever be a part of my life, but it was. The names in this story have been changed.

At the age of 21while living in Atlanta, I was sitting in my church listening to the sermon. I looked behind me and saw a strikingly handsome guy. Leaning over to my mom I whispered, "This is the man I'm going to marry." At the end of the service, we met walking out the door.

He said, "I normally don't walk out this door."

I replied, "I normally don't walk this slowly."

We immediately started dating and the romance began. His name was Craig. He had thick, brown hair with soft, chocolate eyes. He stood about six feet tall and drove a brand new gray Z28. In the early eighties, that was a pretty hot car to own.

After a year of dating, he proposed. We set our wedding date and reserved the chapel. I was about to order invitations when Craig decided he wasn't ready to get married. I couldn't believe it when he backed out of the wedding. I was devastated!

He decided to move to Baton Rouge, Louisiana. He was very vague about why he was moving there. He said he still loved me, but the timing was not right for him.

Once in a while, the phone rang. When I said hello, some-one hung up. I knew it was him. It actually was a comfort to know he was still thinking of me. He came from a difficult childhood and had some baggage from his experience. I just didn't realize to what degree he had been affected.

I dated a few people in the next couple of years, but noth-ing serious. I also became a flight attendant during that time. I moved to Raleigh, North Carolina for a year but I missed Atlanta, so I decided to move back. I would still be based in Raleigh, resulting in a commute to work.

On one of my trips, I flew with a flight attendant named Jennifer. We had a great time flying together, engaging in deep conversation on the jumpseat. She called me her little psychol-ogist. Then it dawned on her: She had a cousin who lived in Atlanta named Matt. He was going to school to become a clini-cal psychologist. It would be the perfect blind date.

I had been on only one blind date before and it was a fiasco. I couldn't wait for it to be over. Needless to say, I was a little hesitant about going on another, but I agreed.

When I opened the door, I immediately felt attracted to him. He was the opposite of Craig. He stood six feet two inches tall. He had wavy, light brown hair, blue-green eyes, and fair skin. The chemistry between us was electrifying. We dated for about two or three years. During that time I began to feel like more of a wife than a girlfriend; however, there was one problem: I had no ring on my finger.

I was ready to get married, but I felt Matt distancing himself from me. I told him we've been dating each other long enough to know which direction this was heading. He mentioned an old college girlfriend was writing him letters and he still had feelings for her. A twinge of pain shot through me. I told him I wouldn't want to marry him only to find out five years down the road that he was still fantasizing about his old girlfriend. "Go back to her and figure it all out," I suggested.

She came from a wealthy family and lived in Germany. He flew over there and brought her back to the States. It was surreal. I thought the odds of him coming back to me were slim. I knew the best thing I could do now was to move on with my life. A little fun in the sun was just what the doctor ordered and thought Florida might be a good choice to look for a condo or townhouse.

It's funny in life when you think you are heading in a certain direction, something comes up and prevents you from heading that way. I call it fate, but in this case it was disaster.

I hadn't been to church for quite a while. One particular Sunday something kept telling me to go. During the service, I needed to use the restroom. On the way, I noticed a handsome man sitting casually on a desk in the back of the congregation. I thought I wouldn't have a chance with this guy, but gave him my best flirtatious smile and walked by.

As I returned, I heard a voice that said, "Chris?"

I glanced over and gasped, "Craig?"

"Are you married?" he asked hesitantly.

"No, are you?"

"No," he said quietly. He had changed in the past five years; perhaps even more handsome. I went from a brunette to a blonde, so I know I looked different.

I thought this was fate. Matt going back to his old girlfriend and now here I am with my old boyfriend. We picked up right where we left off. Craig read his Bible often and expressed some of his personal interpretations of scripture that were, in my mind, a little too extreme. But he was genuinely interested in helping others, especially people who were down and out. I was touched by that.

We always had nicknames for each other. Mine was Kiki, and his was Cigi. He was so protective of me. He worried about me going out at night and always made me feel very secure. I received a steady stream of romantic notes and letters. They all seemed to end with the word forever. Anyone would have fallen for him.

In fact, he said there were several girls in church who were interested in him. One Sunday after the sermon, a young woman came running after us. She was a beautiful brunette dressed immaculately. Brazenly, she stood in front of me and asked him why he hadn't called. I was a little embarrassed for him, but secretly felt honored I was the one he chose.

After a while, Craig began to open up with me. He said he was fired from his last job. I never got a clear understanding why. All I know is he took me to his previous employer's office around midnight one night and was copying some papers. It looked like personal information. I don't know why I didn't ask more questions, I guess at that point I had no reason to distrust him.

He then confided, "I have had a streak of bad luck this past year. I was temporarily staying with friends and rented a storage unit. Someone broke into the unit and stole most of my clothes and belongings." Full of sympathy, I bought him suits, shirts and ties to interview for work.

He was now living with my parents and me. They loved him. He called them mom and dad and we all gladly tried to help him. Next thing we knew, a collection agency called the house. Craig was behind on payments for his vehicle. This was so foreign to me. I always had spotless credit. He charmed the person on the phone until they were laughing like old buddies. Ultimately, the charm wore off and mom and dad ended up covering his payments and insurance. We still loved him and thought he was just having a difficult time. He was pressuring me to get married, but I told him not until he had a job.

Six months had now passed. I often wondered how Matt was doing. One day I went to get the mail. Before I reached in the mailbox, I had a sense that something might be in there from Matt. That is how strong our connection was. I sifted through the mail and there was the letter. He said he had made a big mistake. The relationship with his girlfriend in Germany was over and he was now ready to be the perfect husband. I had strong feelings for him, but the resentment was still there. I told him Craig and I were planning to marry. He was devastated, but I forged ahead, determined to ignore my feelings for him.

Eventually, Craig did get a job. He said it was a growing company and could see himself being vice president in no time at all. He would sell computers in the Southeast region making a good salary plus commission. The best part of all, the company was going to give him a car. We could sell his automobile and save some money. I certainly wasn't marrying him for his financial status. I loved him because he was, so I thought, such a great guy. All of that changed immediately the day I said, "I do."

I have great benefits with my job. One of which is flying for free. We planned a Hawaiian ocean sunset wedding in Maui, but thought we could save money on airfare for him if we legally got married before we went. A town called Ringgold, Georgia, was renowned for couples who wanted a quick wedding (sort of like a mini Las Vegas). I don't know if it was nerves or what, but when the preacher said, "We are *all* gathered here," it struck me as hilarious because there were only three of us standing there. I unsuccessfully suppressed laughter throughout the entire ceremony. As it turned out, the joke was on me.

On the way to Maui, I saw an immediate change in Craig. He became moody and sullen. He had always been a ladies man; maybe he was feeling a little trapped. I soon started making a lot of excuses for his behavior.

When we got to Maui, we unpacked and decided to go for a hike. We climbed some cliffs at the far end of the island. Craig slipped and fell and was in obvious pain. I gathered ice from the cooler, wrapped it in a towel, and put it on his leg. "Get that f---ing ice off my leg, Chris." he ranted. I told him he needed to reduce the pain and swelling. He replied, "I came out here to get some G---D--- sun, and I am going to lay out here until I get it." I was shocked. He had never used such language in my presence nor talked to me that way. *Who was this guy?* I lay there speechless and sick at heart. His skin was turning pink from the sun when he announced, "Okay, let's go." I drove him to the hospital in silence. The ER physician said Craig tore some ligaments in his leg, prescribed pain meds and sent him back to the hotel on crutches.

Due to the circumstances, we cancelled the wedding. After all, we were legally married. My mom and dad (our witnesses) were the only ones who were going to attend. The wedding coordinator who arranged the ceremony felt so sorry for us she gave us a refund.

Craig and I were staying in a condo a couple of miles from Kaanapali, a beautiful complex with luxurious hotels land-scaped with gorgeous waterfalls and lush gardens.

As we were walking along the path, I stopped Craig. "This would be a perfect place to take pictures."

"I am not in the mood to take pictures, Chris." He snapped back with a sullen expression. *No big deal.* I shrugged it off. We continued walking.

I noticed a girl in a thong bikini parading around as if she were the hottest thing ever. I am the one who said, "Craig, look over there." He looked and looked at her and kept staring as she disappeared around the corner. Obviously, he was trying to get to me. I whispered, "Craig, you are on your honeymoon." He sneered and limped off. I wasn't going to let him bother me, so I continued taking pictures of the graceful swans swimming nearby.

I meandered out to the parking lot where the jeep we had rented was parked. The jeep was there, but no sign of Craig. I looked for him everywhere but couldn't find him. I checked in the parking lot again, but this time the jeep was gone. I couldn't believe it! He took off and left me there by myself on our honeymoon.

I sat on the cement median, tears streaming down my face. *What had I done?* Anger soon replaced the tears. Constantly checking my watch, a long wait of forty-five minutes passed. Just before giving up, I saw the jeep coming around the corner. I opened the door and stepped in. I took off the wedding ring (which I co-signed at purchase) and flung it at him, "I want this marriage annulled immediately," I snapped.

"I'm so sorry, Kiki," he soothed. And managed to sweet talk his way out of the situation. I reluctantly agreed to give him another chance and we flew back to Atlanta.

We moved out of my parents' house and rented an apartment in Alpharetta, (a suburb of Atlanta), hoping to save money for our own home. Craig's behavior did not change for the better; in fact, it only worsened. Something was terribly wrong. The promise of a company car did not happen and Craig needed a vehicle. He found a red Bronco. I told him I would finance it through my credit union, thinking that if I had to leave him at some point in time, I could sell it.

After a couple of months, I noticed my credit cards were getting a hefty balance. "I'll pay you back, I'll pay you back," he grumbled. He never did. While traveling on business, he used my credit cards for expenses.

"Craig, isn't there any way we can get like $10,000?" I asked jokingly one day as I struggled to pay the bills.

"Actually, there is, I know some drug dealers here in Atlanta. I'd have to throw some rocks to shatter the lights and thump a few heads in, but I could take a quarter of a million dollars just like that. They can't do anything because it is drug money," he replied.

My mouth dropped open but I laughed it off and said, "Yeah, right." Inside, I was horrified. *What did he mean, "Thump a few heads in?"*

We stopped attending church, and he didn't want to see my parents anymore. I occasionally drove over to my mom and dad's house during the day, numb and shell-shocked from his escalating verbal abuse and erratic behavior. They were worried about me but didn't know what to do. I told them everything would be fine, knowing nothing would be.

I brought my mom to our apartment for lunch one day not realizing Craig was home. He pulled me aside and yelled, "Don't you ever bring anyone here unless you call first!" It didn't make sense. Why did it matter if I made lunch for my mother? *What was he trying to hide?*

The person who had fiercely protected me while we were dating was gone. My feelings of security were replaced with fear. He could care less if I went out late at night. I am a very strong person, but his need for control was weakening me.

Craig mentioned we should take a trip to the mountains. I thought that was an excellent idea. Maybe a change of scenery would be good for our relationship. He spent a lot of time in the mountains, so I felt safe knowing he would make a great tour guide. We drove and drove and ended up in a very remote area. I hoped he might take me to a beautiful park or waterfall. He stepped out of the SUV and I followed him to the back. He opened the rear door and pulled out a huge machete. He slowly lifted the knife above his head and slowly brought it down. I had a horrible feeling.

"What are you going to do with that, Craig?" I quietly asked, determined to show no fear.

"I'm just going to clear the path." He glanced at me with a dark look that sent chills up my spine.

He paused and stood there. Was he trying to intimidate me, scare me or could he actually hurt me? How could I feel that way about my own husband? I immediately tried to dismiss those thoughts, but they were there. We walked into the woods and hiked for several hours. I kept a wary eye on the machete. We returned home, but I never forgot the implied threat from that day.

One night Craig came home and said a guy who works with him was a hit man and an arsonist on the side. Again, I'm sure my mouth dropped.

"Craig, I hang around people who are like me. What are you doing hanging around someone like that?" I asked. "Aren't you afraid of what he might do to you if you make him mad?"

He replied, "Chris, he thinks I am the craziest guy there is. No, I am not afraid of him."

If this thug thinks my husband is the craziest person there is, what has he done to earn his respect? Another red flag, but I brushed it off.

After about three months, Craig asked if I was sure we had rental insurance on our apartment. I wondered why he was asking because nearly everything we had was mine. The next day, I stopped by my insurance company. I told them I wanted the insurance policy in my name only. If something were to happen to me, at least he wouldn't collect anything.

Two days later, he was talking on the phone and something upset him. He yanked the phone out of the wall and threw it over the balcony. You didn't want to tick him off. Another time we were sleeping in bed. He pulled the cover from me onto him. I pulled it back on me. He jumped out of bed and yelled, "You better hope that was worth it." He slammed the door. *Worth what,* I thought. Is he going to come in here and kill me because of a blanket? It was crazy! He was crazy!

I could hear him frequently conning people on the phone. "Yeah, I am going to stay home and work on the computer," he told his boss. We didn't have a computer at the time. He looked for ways to cut corners or get away with something. I repeatedly told him, "Just do the right thing, Craig, just do the right thing." He never did.

The last and final blow came after four months. He said, "Maybe we should consider getting more life insurance." I felt the air being sucked out of me. I didn't ask why he wanted more life insurance. I had learned by then not to ask why. Besides, I knew he would lie. And the truth was, I knew the answer. Everything in me thought my husband was going to kill me. As soon as I could get away without suspicion, I left and went directly to an attorney and explained my situation. He said, "You better get out immediately. I've seen this happen over and over. When he goes on his sales trip to North Carolina, you take your things and get out."

A week later, Craig drove to North Carolina. The spare bedroom was considered Craig's. He said I wasn't supposed to go in there, so I didn't. But today I needed to know what was in there. Mom and I went over to the apartment armed with a camera. We opened the door and crept in. Behind the door was something that looked like a rifle in a camouflage bag. I thought perhaps it was a hunting rifle. Mom said, "Well go ahead and get it out." I slowly pulled out a silver barrel machine gun. I was shocked! A huge chest was in the closet. I opened it to find three handguns. One appeared to be fake. I found a special agent badge, dynamite sticks with nails attached to them, and a sack full of ammunition. Three sets of nun-chucks echoed, *"Thump a few heads in."* We left the room and quickly loaded up most of the belongings that were mine, but still left a lot of my possessions for him. I even bought him a new set of dishes and silverware. I thought somehow it might diminish his rage when he found out I was gone.

I temporarily moved back in with my parents. My mom, dad and I sat paralyzed on the couch. "What is going to happen when he finds out I left? What is he going to do?" We about jumped out of our skins when the phone rang knowing it was him. I slowly picked up the phone.

He said, "Hey, my airline travel card is missing!" (At the time, you needed this to travel on standby.)

"Are you sitting down, Craig? I've got something important to say. You're no husband, I am no wife. You are a psychopathic liar, a con artist, a sociopath..." I don't remember what else I said; I told it like it was.

He said, "Wow, no one has ever really known me like you."

I asked, "Have you killed anyone?"

He sarcastically said, "I've shot people, Chris, I haven't killed anyone."

Whether he was trying to get a reaction from me or not, I instinctively believed him. I vividly recall Craig's fixation when lone women walked by on the street. It didn't matter if they were attractive or not; I just remember his intense look. It scared me.

I tried to cover all the bases and cancelled my credit cards. The time I spent with Craig left me with a debt of $26,000. I didn't have any idea how long it would take to pay that off. There was only one card I had forgotten about. He used it to purchase a television and VCR shortly after our conversation.

Then the stalking began. Every couple of hours each day, the phone rang. Some days he was the good old Cigi I loved.

Other days he would say, "you b----, you c---, no one has ever walked out on me." I considered going to the police and getting a restraining order, but I knew it wouldn't matter if I had one. He said he was above the law. He had no conscience and felt justified in what he did: that was all that mattered.

I told him the Bronco he was driving was legally mine, and I could take it at any time.

"If you lay a finger on this vehicle, you and your family will pay," he threatened. "You consider that a warning, Chris."

Another big debt! I just couldn't let him have it. I was already in enough trouble financially. I told him he could keep it as long as he paid me a $200 payment each month. This was music to his ears. He, of course, wouldn't send the payment; he insisted on giving it to me in person. It was yet another opportunity to torture me verbally. One time, he stuck his foot in front of the tire so I couldn't leave after he paid me. Another time, he made me get in the car with him and drove so recklessly I thought he might kill us. He tried anything to get to me. I never let it. At times, I forced myself to cry. For some reason that stopped the torment and led to an apology saying that I didn't deserve it.

He became increasingly volatile. He said there were some bullets with our names on it. At times, my parents and I stared out the window all night wondering if he was going to come.

Other nights we stayed in hotels to feel safe. One time he said, "Maybe you would know what it's like to lose a wife if you didn't have any of your things." We thought maybe he was going to burn down the house.

After a particularly bad conversation with him, I was terrified to remain in Georgia. Mom and I escaped to my sister's house in North Dakota. Unfortunately, this meant leaving my dad all alone in Atlanta. Because I wasn't answering the phone, Craig came to my parents' front door to see where I was. Dad wouldn't tell him, so Craig said, "Yeah, I heard Chris found my guns." He was indirectly threatening my poor dad. My father is the kindest man you will ever meet. He wouldn't hurt a fly. Dad ultimately told Craig where I was and the phone rang at my sister's house. When I answered, he was surprisingly conciliatory. Because mom and I had jobs, we had to return to Atlanta.

I began flying as much as I could, partly to pay off the debt but mainly for the safety of my parents. I figured if I wasn't home, he wouldn't harass them. My dad locked their bedroom door with his 35-year-old gun next to the bed at all times. I felt awful putting them through that. They both worked, so at times I was all alone in the house.

During one of those days of solitude, I heard someone knocking on the front door. Of course I knew who it was. The knocking turned to pounding. I didn't know what to do, so I pretended like I had been washing my face. I answered the door wiping my wet face with a towel.

"What's going on out here?" I asked.

"You better open up that door," he raved. "I am not responsible for how I am when I get mad, Chris."

For the next four months, I had to be very careful not to react the wrong way, say the wrong thing, get angry, show selfishness, have weakness, and definitely not make him feel that life was not worth living for him or for me. I had to stay one step ahead of him at all times. Some of the words that came from me were those of a higher power, not my own. He threatened suicide and said there would be a note in the left-hand side of the drawer. All night long I wondered whether his plans included me. The next morning, the phone inevitably rang.

I reminded him reading his Bible used to give him comfort — why not try that? He said in a raspy voice, "I roll my joints with Bible pages, Chris." *What did that mean? Drugs, maybe it was all about drugs.* Actually, at this point I didn't know what to think.

I went to church next Sunday and saw Matt up in the balcony. I sat down next to him. I said that his "big mistake" was nothing compared to mine. I told him briefly my situation and I was getting an annulment. He said he had met someone else, and was getting married in a couple of months. We looked at each other with great sadness. The chemistry was strikingly familiar.

Craig told me he was getting Ted Turner's lawyer to fight the annulment. It was hard to know when he was bluffing or when he was telling the truth. In this case he must have been bluffing, because he never showed up to contest the annulment. *Thank goodness it was over* or so I thought.

The pay phone continued to ring even in my operations area at the airport. Flight attendants called themselves my personal telephone service because the phone was always for me. This was before cell phones were a part of our existence.

Craig told me he met his next victim. (He used the word "victim".) *Is that what he thought when he met me?* I asked what she was like. He said, "She's 29 years old, beautiful, and owns two hotels." Some of the things Craig said were fabricated, some weren't. It made it difficult to know what to believe. He said he was going to disappear like a phantom and take the Bronco with him.

Toward the end of the ordeal, I hadn't dated anyone, though I was granted the annulment. I knew I was still in danger and had been very cautious about dating. I met a young man named John whom I enjoyed talking with and who made me laugh. I forgot what it was like to feel lighthearted. He asked me if I would like to go to an AT&T tennis tournament. Jimmy Connors was playing. I told him my situation and the danger he might be in, but he said he would take the chance.

Craig called earlier that day. He wanted to come over because he had his payment for me. Knowing I couldn't tell him I had a date, I told him I needed to buy a gift for Mother's Day.

That evening just as John and I were about to get on the interstate, Craig turned off. I can't remember why, but we were driving my car. The look on Craig's face was pure evil when he saw John. "Put the pedal to the metal," I told him urgently. "We are in trouble!"

I called mom and told her I had just seen Craig and I didn't know what is going to happen. Thirty minutes later, he was on her doorstep.

"She lied to me," he told my mother.

"You put her in a no-win situation, Craig," my mom replied. "If she told you she was out with someone, you would go ballistic just like you are doing now."

"Well, I am not going to give her another dime," he huffed.

My mom's very last words to him were, "At least she has always paid what she owes."

That incident was on a Thursday night. I called him the next morning asking if he were okay. "I'm okay, but I'm not okay," he muttered. "I need to see you tomorrow before your trip to Madrid. Meet me at the bank; I have some money for you." I hung up the phone shaking. I had to do what he said. I knew he needed to have some kind of control. I needed to trust my instincts.

I pulled into the bank's parking lot. I waited for a long time feeling uneasy, not sure what to expect. The red Bronco pulled into the lot. My heart began to race. My hands shook as I rolled down the window.

"Early as usual," I said in a kidding voice.

I knew this situation needed to be played very carefully. He spit his gum on my windshield.

"Oh that's real cute, Craig," I said. He picked it off and threw it on the ground.

"Here is the money that I owe you." He threw $75 at me.

I said, "Thank you."

"I owe you another $25." he stated.

"That's okay, just keep it." I couldn't show any signs of being selfish.

"Get out of the car, Chris." *That's it, he is going to kill me right here at the bank.* I got out of the car.

He hugged me, kissed me and said, "Goodbye forever, Chris."

I drove off stunned. All kinds of thoughts were going through my head. *Is he going to be a phantom and disappear? Well, there goes the truck. Surely he won't do anything foolish.*

I came home Monday night from my trip to Madrid. *Hmm, no phone calls. That was strange.* All day Tuesday the phone did not ring. Now I was beginning to think something happened. *Had he disappeared as he promised?*

Later that day, my insurance agent called and said Craig didn't pay his insurance policy for the truck. They were forced to cancel the policy. I told her that figures. "I will call him to straighten it out."

Craig had assured me he was paying all of his bills for the last four months. I told him I wanted my wedding ring so I could sell it and pay off the financing. He said he wanted to give it to his next wife and would continue making the payments. Unfortunately, he never did.

I called Craig on Wednesday. I called and called, but there was no answer. I telephoned his office. His boss said he hadn't been in all week. "He'd better show up sometime soon or he's fired," she said. A wave of uncertainty hit me. *Maybe he hadn't disappeared; maybe it was something far worse.* About three weeks prior to this, Craig told me he was going to leave the company he was working for and take them for at least a thousand dollars before he left. I wasn't sure of his plans or if he indeed had done so.

I felt compelled to drive to the apartment. On the way there, I considered two possibilities: his Bronco is not parked in the lot indicating he has probably disappeared or if his Bronco is there, he may have done the unthinkable and killed himself.

Turning the corner, I saw the red Bronco. I slowly walked up to the apartment door noticing all of the windows were open. I knocked on the door, with no answer in return. "Craig, Craig, Are you in there?" I heard nothing. I knew in my heart that it was over.

I drove back to mom and dad's house. I guess I wasn't mentally prepared to enter the apartment yet. While driving home, everything seemed to be in slow motion. I can still hear what songs were playing on the radio. I can still tell you which stop sign I missed.

I called mom at work and said, "He is in there."

"I will meet you there," she said.

I called John, the innocent guy who took me to the tennis match. He said, "I'm sure he's okay, but I am coming with you."

When John and I arrived, we went directly to the apartment manager's office. I explained the situation to her. She called one of her employees and the four of us went to the apartment together.

We walked in tentatively. Nothing seemed to be out of place. The windows were open, so there wasn't an odor. *Maybe I was wrong.* The door to his 'secret' room was closed. John was the first to open it. "Oh my God," he said. "He is in there." Craig had taken off all of his clothes then shot himself in the right-hand side of the head. He lay face down in a pool of blood.

We called the police. It took three hours for them to do their investigation. One of the police officers held something out in his hand. "Do you know what this is?" I shook my head no. He said it was a homemade hand grenade. "What would he be doing with that?" I told him that was the Craig I didn't know. There was no note.

Mom arrived, and in silence we tearfully watched them carry Craig's body off in a bag. My heart was full of mixed emotions. Part of me knew if he were living, I would never be free. But part of me mourned the person I once loved. The hardest thing I had to do was call his family. How do you tell a mother her son is no longer here? Stunned and devastated, she requested his body be flown to where he grew up. She also said she wanted me to come to the funeral. I never told his family the whole story.

The next day I went to the apartment to pick out his favorite suit for the funeral. It was a rainy and dreary day. I drove in a daze the whole way. While stopped at a light, I heard a tremendous crash behind me. The next thing I knew, my head slammed against the steering wheel. The change compartment spewed coins everywhere. *This can't be happening.* I pulled over.

Two cars behind me were badly mangled. The driver, who rear-ended my car, apologized and gave me his insurance card. The back end of the car was damaged, but I was too distraught to mess with it. I never did call his insurance company. My mom was driving a mile behind me. She hoped the ruckus ahead did not involve me, but unfortunately it did. Once the police report was filled out, I drove off and headed for the apartment.

I opened the apartment door and we about gagged. Because of the weather conditions outside, the windows were now closed. The putrefying smell was worse than any dead animal. My mom and I slowly opened the door where Craig shot himself. The blood soaked carpet had an imprint where his head had lain. I grabbed his favorite suit, tie, and shoes.

I flew to his childhood home for the funeral. I was standing with his brother over Craig's casket. I pointed out a scar on his hand and shared Craig's version of how he got it. His brother just laughed. He said that he and Craig were horsing around when they were young and he had put his hand through the screen door. Not exactly the tale I heard. It was just one of many eye opening comments that day.

His old girlfriend was present. She was also a flight attendant for another airline. "You are one lucky girl to be alive," she said. Craig had beaten her up so severely that she was placed in intensive care. He had falsely accused her of cheating on him. He was in her apartment when she came home one day and started hitting her. She ran into the closet waiting until she heard his footsteps leave. When she thought he was gone, she opened the door only to find him still there. He almost beat her to death.

I came home from the memorial exhausted. Mom and dad told me a certified letter was sent to their house. It stated that Craig owed a lot of money to the IRS. If he did not pay it within fifteen days, he would be thrown in jail. He must have known this from prior notices. Now things made more sense. Craig kept urging me to stick with him for six more months and not pursue the annulment. "Just six more months," he said. Maybe it was because he wanted me to be responsible for his debts as a wife. I remember him saying coming from a Christian background, I could never leave him. Thank God I had the strength to leave.

I was in a lot of trouble financially. I remembered Craig saying he put my name as the beneficiary of his $25,000 life insurance policy with his company. I knew it was probably null and void because it was suicide, but I was desperate, so I called his boss. We talked intimately about everything. She said Craig always said his region in North Carolina was a gold mine. His papers showed nothing. She didn't know what he was doing. She told me the best thing I could do is to put everything behind me.

I went with mom and dad to visit some relatives in Illinois. While driving home to Georgia, I felt something might be waiting for me. I didn't know what, but it wasn't a feeling of dread. As I approached the house, I reached with anticipation into the mailbox. I was hoping something good was in there, but nothing of interest was inside. I usually can trust my intuition, so I hurriedly entered the house. There, was the blinking answering machine. I immediately replayed the messages. There was one from his boss informing me the insurance policy went through. I jumped up and down with joy. I called Craig's boss. She asked if I would repay Craig's thousand-dollar loan and some other miscellaneous debts. I thought back to Craig's conversation. "I am going to leave this company and take them for at least a thousand dollars." I said absolutely and thanked her profusely. It paid off most of the debt. The only things left were the emotional scars.

14

Goodbye Forever, but Not Quite Gone

$\mathscr{D}$eath is part of life, but what about life after death? For those of you who think death is final and there's nothing beyond, you may want to skip this chapter. I am going to tell my own personal story following Craig's suicide. During the stalking days, he said, "I am going to haunt you forever." He indeed did!

While I was attending Craig's funeral, I went to his childhood park to be by myself. I felt I wasn't alone, though. I sat on a swing gently rocking and said out loud, "If you're here, I want you to move that empty swing back and forth." I looked and looked. Nothing happened. *Whew! He's gone.*

About a week after the funeral, my family gathered around our dining room table. We were talking about the whole unbelievable nightmare. You go through so many emotions when something like this happens: denial, responsibility, relief, guilt, etc. I kept feeling a slight breeze touch my arms. After the third time, I looked to see if the ceiling fan was on, but it wasn't. My mom asked what was wrong, saying I looked spooked. I shrugged it off.

I continued working high time. That means you work your schedule plus you pick up other flight attendants' trips they don't want to fly. I was seldom home and was temporarily living at my parents' house. I am guessing I was only there maybe five or six days a month.

Once, I walked in the kitchen and a gentle breeze touched my face. I didn't think much of it. I briefly smelled a putrid odor that was like the one in the apartment — reminiscent of a dead animal. It lasted a second or two.

I was in the kitchen putting some dishes in the dishwasher. All of a sudden, a loud, knocking noise occurred directly underneath my feet. It sounded like, da, da, da, da. I felt it and heard it. I jumped up and looked under the cabinet, but nothing was out of place. The dishwashing soap, window cleaner and bleach were still upright. I went down in the basement and looked up to where I was standing. There were no pipes or anything else that could have caused that ruckus. My parents still worked, so I was home alone during the day. I called mom to see if anything like that ever happened to her; she said no. "I'm sure it's nothing," she replied. This reassured me a little.

The next morning, I was taking a shower. A heavy, gold-plated razor fell off the edge of the tub. I thought that was strange. Out of curiosity, I put direct water pressure on the razor. It didn't budge.

I was halfway through curling my hair when I heard the vent above my head move by itself. It's the kind where you move your thumb to adjust the flow. I heard it turn slowly, urrrrrh. A drop of dirty water fell to the floor. I felt an eerie feeling as if someone were staring at me. I hurried with my hair and ran out of the house to call mom. I explained to her what happened. She said, "Listen, even if it is him, you didn't let him control you when he was here; don't let him control you when he's gone. Don't pay any attention."

I went on my trip to Madrid. One of the other flight attendants was getting married. She said she was in need of a wedding veil. I had one I never used and asked if she would be interested in seeing it. To which she replied, "Absolutely." When I returned home from my trip, I began to search for the veil. It was down in the basement (along with everything else that once belonged to Craig).

While looking for the veil, I found some old pictures of Craig and me on our "honeymoon". I was thumbing through them when suddenly the light went out. It was now pitch black. I blindly felt around for the string that turned the light on. When

I finally found it, I gave the string a firm tug. The light came on. I found the veil and scurried upstairs as fast as I could. Being a logical person, I thought it didn't make any sense. If the light was on and the bulb went off, when I pulled the string to turn it on, it should have clicked off first.

Mom and I were sitting in the living room having a conversation. It was supposed to be a private one. I told her there was a pilot who asked me out, but I wasn't ready to date anyone. Suddenly, we heard two loud knocks on the window. The chance a bird could have struck the window two simultaneous times was pretty slim. We were on the second floor, so there was no way anyone could have been outside the window. Besides, the knocks sounded like they came from the inside. We looked at each other and shook our heads. If you let your imagination control you, fear will get the best of you. We continued on with our conversation and tried to ignore anything else.

At this point, I was a little afraid to go to bed at night. I always had the television on so I wouldn't hear anything. Eventually, I would fall asleep then turn off the television somewhere in the middle of the night. One time, I did just that. I woke up from a deep sleep, turned off the TV, but this time I didn't go back to sleep. I looked around feeling uneasy and felt a heavy presence slowly lowering itself on top of my legs. I lay there rigid with fear and said out loud, "If you're here

Craig, you need to go to the light." That is what I had heard you should say in this situation.

I had a trip to London and told the crew everything that was going on including the mysterious night visitor. We were at the hotel getting ready to leave for the airport. The bus driver was loading our luggage. I was the last crew member to get on the greyhound bus. As I took the first step on the bus, the radio turned itself on full blast. The crew was totally spooked because no one was in the driver's seat. Whether it was a co-incidence or not, many of the crewmembers said jokingly they didn't want to fly with me anymore.

Meanwhile, back at home, the newest revelation was doors locking by themselves. Mom and dad did not know they had a lock on their master bedroom door. We heard crashes in the garage and in the basement. Under investigation, nothing seemed to be out of place.

Our entire family had gathered for a couple of days for the Thanksgiving holiday. We were having a conversation when my sister-in-law mentioned she had gone to the same school I did when we were children. This was the first I heard of that, so I told her I would go in the basement and see if I could find my childhood class pictures. I asked if anyone was brave enough to go with me; my brother reluctantly volunteered. After finding the pictures, we ran up the stairs as fast as we could. To our amazement, the kitchen door was locked and we couldn't get in the kitchen. We banged and banged on the door. At first we thought someone was playing a joke on us, but no one in our family locked it.

I did see something only one time. I went to sleep with the television on, and then of course later on, turned it off. In the corner of the room, I saw something that caught my eye. The best way I can describe it is it looked like a glowing, day old, deflated balloon. I just turned off the TV and thought maybe my eyes were playing tricks on me. (You know when you look at the sun, you can still see its shadow if you close your eyes.) I closed my eyes and didn't see anything. I slowly opened them, but it was still there. It hovered for a second or two, and then slowly moved in front of my closet where it disappeared. What was strange about this incident was I heard a non-audible voice say, "Thanks for giving my brother my ties" — which I had done after the funeral.

I moved out of my parents' house after a year. I moved into my own little apartment in Buckhead, a suburb of Atlanta. I never heard or felt anything even though I lived by myself. My parents, on the other hand, did continue to hear things for quite a while. They eventually sold their house and moved back to the country in Illinois.

15

Movie Stars

The most common question I am asked is this: "Have you had any celebrities on board?"

My all-time favorite was Dolly Parton. Wearing a white, fringed outfit, she was an absolute delight and down to earth. Her waist was so small; her breasts were so large and her smile, radiant. She was traveling with her assistant who was as pleasant as she was. I was working first class and gave Dolly her tray. She ate the meat and salad and left behind the bread and dessert. Now, that is will power. I told her she was a very pretty lady. "Well, you are too, sugar," she replied.

I had Cher on board when she was filming the movie "Suspect." She mentioned she had three homes, one in Canada, one in New York and one is LA and probably travels more than I do. I glanced at her script for the movie. It was enormous. I had a newfound respect for what actors go through to learn their lines for a movie. I served her a club soda and she curled her legs and gently rocked back and forth as she stared out the window. She was quietly elegant.

Years later, I saw Tony Bennett sitting on a VIP shuttle cart waiting to catch his flight. I smiled at him, and he flashed his twinkling eyes at me. Knowing that opportunities don't come along like this very often, I had to go over and talk to him. I thanked him for being a part of my Christmas every year with his music. There are certain men I would go out with no matter how old they are; he would be one of them. Jimmy Stewart would have been another.

My favorite male celebrity was Terry Bradshaw. What a great guy! He was an animated talker who used his hands liberally to speak. As I walked by him he accidentally hit my breast. He did this two times. The third time I walked by he said, "Hey come here, I forgot to do something." We both laughed.

I had George Straight on my flight before he became a popular country star. He was traveling from Dallas to San Antonio and was my only passenger in first class. We sat and talked the whole way. He lovingly spoke of his wife and two children.

Toby Maguire and his girlfriend (now wife) were traveling together in first class. He was extremely nice and had impeccable manners, always saying please and thank you. My nephew who is a huge "Spiderman" fan was happy to hear that.

Katie Couric and her late husband, Jay, were boarding the flight from San Juan to Miami years ago. She gave me a big, classic Katie smile and I thought to myself, *"I could be friends with her."*

The flight attendants like to hide behind the gate check-in area while waiting for the incoming airplane to arrive and the passengers deplane. Otherwise we get bombarded with questions about peoples' travel plans. As we were hiding behind the desk in Orlando, Kirstie Alley and her two kids were also trying to find a place to escape. I happened to look up to see her peeking around the corner. I motioned her to join us. She had lost weight and looked great. I loved her personality and told her she could hide out with us anytime.

Jane Fonda boarded my flight and sat in coach by the window. Some movie stars like to be recognized and some don't. Miss Fonda had her sunglasses on, so I assumed she did not want to be bothered. Several passengers asked if I would get her autograph, but I knew it was a bad idea and said no. I looked at her as I passed through the cabin with the beverage cart. From where I was standing, I could only see her from behind. She was shaking her head back and forth. It looked as though she was talking to herself. I jokingly told the other flight attendant I thought she had gone crazy. We finished the service and out of curiosity I had to take a second look at her.

I walked through the aisle picking up the trash, so I wouldn't look conspicuous. She had a piece of paper in her hand and was reading from it. *Aah haa!* She wasn't crazy after all, and was preparing for a speech or studying a script. At the end of the flight, we were preparing the cabin for landing. Miss Fonda stopped me with a finger pointing up. I waited as she finished her water and then her cranberry-apple juice. She looked at me and gave me a wink and a nod of the head. I gave her a wink and a nod in return. I knew without saying a word she appreciated being left alone.

While watching Hoda and Kathie Lee do their morning talk show, I admired Hoda's dress. Later that day, I was walking through the Palm Beach airport terminal and saw Hoda wearing that same dress coming my way.

I said, "Hey, It's nice to see you."

She said, "It's nice to see you, too." I could tell she was as genuine in real life as she was on her television show.

I would like to share even more intriguing morsels from encounters other flight attendants have shared about the rich and famous. You might be surprised to learn that quite a few celebrities aren't so nice off camera. But some things are best left unsaid and the experiences are not first hand and I would not want to gossip. *Yes I would!*

16

Male Thong

My best friend Melanie and I decided to take a vacation for a few days in Cancun, Mexico. Cancun is basically one strip of gorgeous oceanfront hotels. The water is a beautiful turquoise color with thunderous waves. After taking a brisk walk along the beach, Melanie and I decided to get some sun by the pool. Our hotel had a luxurious pool with a three tiered lounging deck. We decided to grab a chair on the top platform.

The best part about lying out by the pool is, of course, getting a beautiful golden tan. The second best thing is people watching. While Melanie and I were checking out the sights, we were delighted to see a juicy specimen walk by. A man in a black thong sashayed to the pool bar. I was amazed! I had never seen a guy with his butt cheeks showing. He was proud as a peacock and full of confidence. We watched and giggled.

He gazed around the pool to find the perfect place to lounge and spotted a chair on the deck below us. We tried not to look but couldn't help ourselves. He shifted to the left and then to the right finally settling in on his stomach. To our amazement, his little "testies" plopped out of his thong. We laughed so hard we cried. He must have realized it was a little breezy down there, because when we looked again they were tucked away safe and sound.

17

My Angel

*A*long time ago, I was working on a 727 aircraft as the coach galley flight attendant. Our airplane was boarding, and I was busy setting up my cart when someone caught my attention. I looked up and a face appeared in the little window of the aft door. He had a big, brown mustache and dark, curly hair. He flashed a big friendly smile and waved to me. I waved back and thought to myself, *"I could have some fun with him."*

I walked maybe four to five steps to the window. Some aircrafts can be entered from the rear, a 727 is one of those aircrafts. When I peered into the window, no one was there. In fact, it was pitch black and the stairs were not lowered. It would have taken him eight to ten steps to get down the stairs even if they were lowered. I called the pilots and asked if they had raised the stairs to the back of the aircraft. They said no.

I was puzzled. The captain asked us to prepare for departure. After my pre-flight duties were accomplished, I sat down on my jumpseat and to my surprise a little note was attached to my side of the seat. "To Chris," it said. I opened it up to find a little message saying something to the effect of beware of the riches and materialistic things in life. I asked the flight attendant next to me if she placed it there. She hadn't. I asked if she told anyone else my name on that flight. Again she said no. Was it an angel or perhaps my guardian angel? I'd like to think so.

18

St. Croix

$\mathscr{S}$tephanie and I liked to take short getaway vacations on our days off. One of those trips led us to the island of St. Croix. We stayed for a total of four days at the hotel where the crewmembers usually stay during layovers. We knew the pilots working the airplane to St. Croix and asked if they would like to join us on our adventures for the first day. The first officer said absolutely, but the captain wasn't up for it. We all agreed it was best to have a male escort along. Little did we know how right we were!

We rented a tiny two door car and drove to the opposite side of the island searching for just the right place to eat dinner. We settled on the only place we could find. The food wasn't great, but the rum punches were delicious. Man, were they potent. We stumbled into the car and started singing. We tried to think of all the theme songs to old TV sitcoms. *The Brady Bunch, The Addams Family, The Partridge Family* — just to name a few. We began reminiscing on our younger days. The first officer shared the story of his first sexual experience. It wasn't a warm apple pie like in the movie *American Pie*. It was actually between two seat cushions on the couch. I'm sure he was mortified the next morning for telling us his secret.

Meanwhile, on the way to the hotel, we saw and heard something that sounded like a good time. After parking the car, the three of us casually walked over to where the sparkling lights and action were taking place. When we got closer, we realized all eyes were on us as we accidentally intruded on a genuine Rastafarian party. No other Americans were there. It was too late to turn around, so we agreed to have one rum punch and leave.

A nice looking guy with a thick, long braid kept staring at us. He later made his move. "Which one of you is with him?" he asked. Both of us clung to the first officer. The Rastie took my hand with a smile and walked me out to the dirt dance floor that was surrounded by twinkling lights. I tried to make the best of the situation, so I moved my feet to the reggae music. Actually, I was starting to have a good time when my partner shifted a little too close and began dirty dancing. His body swayed to the left then to the right with his 'you know what' on my leg. All eyes turned on us as the other dancers began to laugh!

Stephanie was trying to help me, but they bumped her away. My sense of panic was igniting when my hero came to the rescue. The first officer grabbed my hand and yanked me off the dance floor. The three of us took off sprinting toward the beach. We ran as fast as we could. As I was running, I could see strange mounds on the sand in the distance. Because it was nighttime, I couldn't be certain. As we approached, we realized the mounds were actually people making out. We couldn't wait to get out of there. After climbing into the car, all three of us sat speechless on the way to the hotel.

The next day the first officer went to work, so Stephanie and I were on our own. We thought we better stay close to the hotel. (I can't imagine why.) While we were doing some duty-free shopping, we noticed an advertisement for parasailing. Neither one of us had ever gone, so we signed up.

We walked to the rickety pier and saw the name of our boat with the captain waving to us. It looked safe enough. I previously observed people parasailing where they stood on the sand as the boat took off lifting them into the air. Here, the boat did all the work for you. The cables gracefully lifted you up and down. The captain was a jolly soul. He prided himself on having the best boat that could sail a person the highest.

At first it was fun riding the waves as the water splashed our faces. But as the boat rocked back and forth in the deepening ocean waves, my nervousness was trumped by fear. I'm not a very good swimmer, so the thought of flying above the ocean scared me.

Thank God Stephanie took her turn first. It looked as though she was having a good time. I waved to her as the crew carefully lowered her safely to the boat. In her words, it was purely awesome. That relieved my fear a bit. The Captain said no worries as he gave out a chuckle. I put my harness on and whoosh, up I went.

Slowly my fear diminished and I opened my eyes to take a peek. *Hey, this isn't so bad.* I saw large sea turtles swimming beneath me. The clear, turquoise water was breathtakingly beautiful. I even saw a stingray floating gracefully. I was amazed at how one could see so clearly through the depths of the ocean. I was now in my glory, thanking God for being able to see such tremendous beauty.

Soon, my bliss turned to sudden anguish. The boat was slowing down. Assuming the worst, I thought something happened to the captain's ship. I was slowly falling. This didn't happen to Stephanie. *What's going on?* I descended lower and lower and was heading straight into the ocean. My feet hit the water first. It was freezing! The water touched my neck. I almost screamed out for help when my harness jerked and I was lifted up to the glorious sky. When the captain reeled me in the boat, everyone was laughing at me. I didn't find it so funny.

We later had a nice dinner and packed our clothes for the trip home. We spoke of where our next exciting adventure would take us. I assured her there would be no parasailing involved.

19

The Naughty Files

$\mathscr{I}$was known as an adventurous flight attendant who enjoyed each and every layover to the fullest. I had fun with the crewmembers, but never crossed the line. But with the horrible tragedy of my first attempt at marriage, I had lost a piece of myself and missed having fun, so I kind of went through a wild and crazy phase for a short time. Okay, maybe a little more than *kind of*. (Family members, please skip this chapter).

I flew international in Miami after I left Raleigh. It was absolutely the most spectacular time of my flying career. The phrase I found myself repeating was, "I can't believe I am getting paid for this."

Taking the double-deck tour bus in London was awesome; cruising on a boat ride down the Seine River in Paris was breathtaking; viewing the northern lights while flying to Alaska was phenomenal; eating wiener schnitzel in Frankfurt was scrumptious. But Rio de Janeiro was the most memorable — and where I got into the most trouble.

Let me describe the main reason for all the madness. There is a delicious drink called Caipiroska or Caipirinha. It is basically straight alcohol, sugar and lime. It tastes similar to lemonade, but after two drinks you are considered legally drunk. It makes you do things you normally would never do.

The most memorable two-day layover in Rio started with our flight crew going to see a cabaret-like show. All twelve crewmembers sat down at a long table eagerly anticipating what was ahead. As I looked around, I noticed the audience dressed elegantly, as if in London seeing a play. I also noticed a mirrored wall with two scantily clad females dancing. Finally, the show began.

A mermaid was first to sing her sweet song, flashing her colorful fin. Next, exotic dancers wearing sparkly sequined costumes and feathered headdresses gyrated through a samba. After the show, most of the crewmembers wanted to turn in for the night, but the first officer and a male flight attendant wanted to continue on with the evening and dance the night away at a discotheque. No one else wanted to go, so I said I would.

We had a great time dancing and trying to communicate with the Brazilians. The guys kept ordering drinks and I gulped them down. Finally, around 2:30 a.m., my head was spinning and I told the guys that I needed to return to the hotel. A few minutes into the cab ride, I threw up. What was especially awful was we had eaten at a churrascaria (a buffet-type place). I felt horrible for the cab driver. The last thing I remember was getting out of the cab. That was it. I totally blacked out!

I woke up the next morning on my side, naked. A man lay next to me, also naked, with his arm around me! I froze. Everything was hazy as I desperately struggled to remember what happened. *Oh my gosh, did a Brazilian follow me back to the hotel? Was it the male flight attendant? No, he was married.* I was hoping, under the circumstances, that it was the single, good-looking first officer. I slowly turned around and breathed a sigh of relief. Thank God, it was the first officer! "Good morning," he said, and tried to kiss me. I was mortified and felt horrible. I was not exactly kissable at the moment. My hair was pasted to my face, and I was sure I looked hideous. I don't know if anything happened that night but he was kind enough to wash out my pants and shirt in the tub and get me on my feet. You'd think I would have learned my lesson from this experience, but nooooo.

On one of my last trips to Rio, we worked an all-night flight arriving at our hotel at 9 a.m. We were exhausted, but some of us decided to crash by the pool. Besides me, only four of the other nine flight attendants came down: two gay males, one straight male, and one straight female. The pool attendant brought over our delicious lemonade drinks. After the third round and being up all night, we were getting a little giddy. After the fourth drink, we were having lime fights. After the fifth one, the security guard came over and kicked us out of the pool area.

We stumbled over to the straight male flight attendant's room. (He had a cabana room overlooking the pool.) I plunked down on the middle of the couch. One gay flight attendant sat next to me, placing my arm under his and the other gay flight attendant did the same on the other side. I put my hand to my mouth and giggled. The straight male and the straight female were 'making out' right in front of us on the bed. When she realized we were there, she screamed for us to get out.

Once again, I woke up the next morning wondering how I got to my room. Thank goodness I was fully clothed this time. A good thing about hanging out with the gay guys: they won't try anything on you.

I had just enough energy to put on my swimsuit and soak up some rays. Eventually, my two gay buddies came down to join me by the pool. I asked how I got to my room. They reminded me our room keys did not have the room numbers on them. We were all too tipsy to ask the front desk but they did know what floor we were on. So, one carried me over his shoulder while the other one tried each room until my key fit. When they found my room, they threw me on top of the bed. Only in Rio!

Montego Bay, Jamaica, was also a notorious place for letting loose. We stayed in an oceanfront hotel, but there were no televisions in our rooms at the time. This forced the pilots and flight attendants to create their own entertainment. Red Stripe beer was the local favorite, and across the street you could pick up a case inexpensively. Because crewmembers are known to be on the frugal side, this was a winning combination.

My most memorable Jamaica layover was with an all-male crew. We flew in on a 727 aircraft with three pilots, two other flight attendants and me. They carried my bags, opened the doors for me, and spoiled me rotten. We checked into the hotel and made plans for the evening. Actually, we all knew what the plan was; it was just a matter of what time.

In no time, we were sitting seaside, enjoying a Red Stripe, having a ball! Again I said to myself, *"I can't believe I am getting paid for this."* We watched the ever changing sky which had a brilliant sunset. A few happy hours later, it was time to turn in.

We took the elevator up and gathered around. Our rooms were on the same floor. We were all still feeling a bit tipsy and rambunctious and I guess we weren't quite ready for the day to end. I ran to the other end of the hall. We were going to have a race! Don't ask me how or why, but the guys stripped off their shorts and underwear leaving their shirts on, as they took their place at the starting line. I was the designated starter, referee and judge, and stood at the finishing line. I paused and then announced, "On your mark, get set, go!" Down the hall they came racing towards me with their privates flapping away. We laughed hysterically. Those were great guys and even better times. It was all just good fun. (Remember, this was a long, long, time ago and I am sure nothing like this goes on today!)

On another oceanfront layover the whole crew decided to unwind from the flight by listening to the waves and playing on the sand. Later on, I desperately had to use the restroom, but the facilities were far away. The captain suggested I go in the ocean. The sunset faded on the horizon and it was getting dark. That sounded like a good idea to me, so I waded into the gentle waves. Next thing you know, I glanced up and in the distance saw the entire crew ripping their clothes off. Full moons were shining everywhere. They jumped into the ocean and frolicked all around me, obviously forgetting the reason why I was there in the first place!

20

The Deposition

$\mathcal{W}$e began boarding the flight from St. Croix to Miami. We only had forty-five passengers, so we were in for an easy trip — or so we thought.

I was the boarding flight attendant, which means I welcome everyone as they enter the airplane. It was almost time to depart when the captain asked me a question, so I went into the cockpit. While I was there, I heard a loud thud. I looked out into the aisle to find a heavy set woman on her knees. I rushed out to her.

"Are you okay?" I asked. She moaned something unintelligible.

I said, "Listen, if you are in that much pain, why don't you stay here in St. Croix and see a doctor?"

"No, no, I need to get to Miami," she insisted.

"Okay, let me help you to your seat." I took her two heavy bags and followed her.

After the safety briefing, I went to check on her. "How are you doing?" I asked.

"Ooh, my ankle."

I told her I would be right back with some ice for her ankle. About a half an hour later, I asked again in a cheerful voice, "How are you?"

"Ooh my knee," she moaned.

"Let me get some ice for your knee."

We finished our breakfast service. As we were picking up, I asked if she would like anything else to drink. "Yes," she said now rather smugly, "I'll have tomato juice, coffee and water." The tone in her voice alarmed me. I thought to myself, *uh-oh, this lady is going to be trouble!*

I alerted the cockpit. "I think this woman is going to sue." Sure enough, as I walked through the cabin, she stopped me. "Excuse me," she said once again with a stern look on her face. "I need you to be my witness." I murmured under my breath, "*Here we go.*"

I asked if she would like a wheelchair when we arrived in Miami. She said that wouldn't be necessary. The captain ordered one anyway. The last I saw she was arguing with the paramedics that she didn't want a wheelchair. They rolled their eyes at me as I passed by.

I wrote down what happened for my records, and stashed it away in my file cabinet. I did not hear anything for about a year and a half. One of our airline's attorneys called my house. "Flight Attendant Churchill, we need you to come to Miami for a deposition." I knew exactly who he was talking about. He said, "I'll have to warn you, this lady has picked a very good attorney. She usually wins her cases."

I was nervous because I had never been to a deposition. I honestly felt this passenger was an opportunist looking to take advantage of the situation. I picked out a professional silk, rust-colored suit, pulled my hair back and put on eye-glasses. I didn't want anyone to think I was a bubble-headed sky waitress.

I flew to Miami on my day off. The number one flight attendant, Nancy, whom I was flying with that day, and I were driven to the deposition. I waited while Nancy testified first. I was nervous but calm at the same time. The passenger, I learned, was suing for hundreds of thousands of dollars. She claimed she hit her mouth, and that the impact forced her to have a root canal since the accident.

After Nancy took her turn, I was escorted into the room for interrogation. There, a long mahogany table was surrounded by eight leather tufted chairs. Occupying three of the chairs was the airline's attorney, the plaintiff's attorney, and a court reporter. Her attorney was a red-headed, sharply dressed woman, and I could tell she was no push over.

Her first question was asked.

"Where do you live?"

"Atlanta," I stated.

"Where in Atlanta?" she asked curtly.

"Buckhead."

I tried to think of her questions beforehand and was counseled that it was best to answer concisely as possible. Yes or no is preferable.

She fired off another question.

"As the number four flight attendant, where are you supposed to be for boarding?"

"My position is at the forward door where I am to welcome the passengers. However, if a seat duplication might arise, I need to rectify the problem at the gate area. If the captain needs me for any reason, I am also to attend to the cockpit at their request."

"Did you take a picture of the hole in the carpet," her attorney asked.

"There was no hole in the carpet."

"How can you be sure there was no hole?" she asked. I explained the cabin service does their checks in the morning, and if there were a hole it would have been written in the maintenance logbook.

She put her glasses on the edge of her nose again, "Can you swear that you saw them do a cabin check that morning?" I am a flight attendant not an airport worker. How was I supposed to be there in the morning monitoring the cabin routine checks?

She said, "Did you see Miss P_____ hit her mouth?"

"No," I responded.

"Did you see her eat her breakfast?"

"No," (Remember, a year and a half has passed.)

"Can you swear that you did not see her eat her breakfast?" she said quickly. I said, "No, I can't, but I do recall she complained about her ankle and then her knee. I also know that she ordered three beverages, hot and cold."

Basically, this is what appeared to have happened. Miss P was walking up the ramp stand with two heavy bags. She was overweight, struggling and couldn't see the steps. When she reached the top step her heel caught, or she simply tripped over it.

The last words her lawyer said to me were, "I'll see you in court in St. Croix." All in all, it was a very nerve racking experience for me. I felt I answered the questions honestly and to the best of my ability. Thank God, I never had to go back and testify.

21

Cuff-em

We were working a flight from Santa Domingo to New York. It seemed like something always happened on that flight.

I was working coach class on an A-300 with a full customer load. A passenger came on board with a long black, scraggly beard. He was rambling in Spanish, speaking very loudly. *What is up with this guy*, I wondered as he passed by me. I didn't realize there truly was something wrong with him. Later, the passenger approached the galley and asked for a drink. "I'm sorry, we can't serve alcoholic drinks on the ground in coach," I stated. "You will have to wait until after we take off." That was the last I saw of him during the boarding process.

After we took off, the first class flight attendants said the passenger stumbled his way up the aisle toward them ranting and demanding a drink. The cockpit door was open because the flight attendants were giving the pilots their beverage. The man drifted toward the cockpit, so the pilots immediately slammed the door shut. Our number one flight attendant, Julio, spoke Spanish and told the passenger he needed to return to his seat immediately. He stormed out of first class and headed back to his seat which, unfortunately, was in my section.

He sat on the aisle in the last row of coach. I had to pass him several times with the meal cart. The first time I passed by him, he kicked my calf. I politely said, "Don't do that." I was thinking to myself, *something is wrong with this guy.* As I was handing out the trays for the meal service, I happened to look toward the rear of the cabin. He was pacing back and forth around the exits. I felt very uneasy, but continued to empty out my meal cart. I made my way toward the galley after depleting the first cart. Luckily, the seatbelt sign was on, so I told him he needed to take his seat. He obeyed while shaking his head back and forth. Again, I passed by him with a full meal cart. He reached over and slapped me on the rear end. I pointed my finger at him and firmly said, "Not one more time."

I called Julio, a big guy who won't take anything from anybody. Marching toward the back of the cabin with great authority, Julio told the ill-behaved passenger to keep his hands to himself and remain seated. Unfortunately, Julio's presence had no bearing on the passenger. He started to lose it and then threatened to kill everyone on the aircraft.

We called the captain and without hesitation he said to cuff him. Julio was elected to do the honors as I held the passenger's hands behind his back. Surprisingly, he offered no resistance. (Two pieces of emergency equipment are required for flight attendants to have with them at all times: a mask used for CPR and plastic cuffs.) For the rest of the flight, the passenger had frequent outbursts and occasionally spit on the floor. Unbeknownst to me, his family was traveling with him. His father and two sisters were sitting two rows ahead of him. They warned us against taking the handcuffs off, for fear he would become violent. Apparently, the man was recently released from a mental facility.

When we landed, security took the passenger off the airplane first. Then the captain and I were taken by car to the New York police precinct office located near the airport. Whenever there is an incident on the aircraft, there is always plenty of paperwork. Because the man was a threat to the cockpit, it became a federal offense. The last I heard while at the office, the passenger was still screaming at the top of his lungs at the police officers.

This happened to me again several years later from Seattle to Miami. Thank God, I was the boarding flight attendant because the following passenger never made it to Miami.

I enjoy taking tickets at the gate. It gives me a chance to welcome everyone on board, and it also gives me a chance to see *who* is coming on board. I was taking a man's ticket when I noticed a foul body odor. I looked up to see where the smell was coming from and saw a tall, lanky passenger with uncombed hair and beard wearing a tattered trench coat. I took his ticket and welcomed him aboard. Following the passenger was a couple on their way to the islands. "You have to keep your eye on that passenger," they advised. "Something is not right with him."

Later on during the boarding process, a father of one of the passengers came up to me clearly shaken. "If that man stays on the aircraft, I am not letting my daughter go." I knew who he was talking about. I asked why he was so concerned.

"He took his tennis racket out of its jacket and pretended like he was shooting everyone at the gate." He also mentioned a couple of other weird behaviors. Because of my previous experience with the unstable passenger on the New York flight, I knew what the implications could be for the next five hours. I informed the agent, the captain, and the number one flight attendant. They all agreed to not take any chances and remove the passenger from the aircraft before we took off.

I watched as the agent approached the passenger. He was cool, calm and collected. We all breathed a sigh of relief when he allowed himself to be escorted off the plane without a fight. The passenger sitting next to him thanked us and said, "Look in his seatback pocket." In that short amount of time, the crazy man was taking our magazines and shredding them. He then took the strips of paper and stuffed the seatback compartment with them.

Thank God, we learned from our previous experience or who knows what story I would be telling you now!

22

Staying Alive

$\mathscr{I}$ have been very fortunate in my career not to have anyone die on my flight. My friend wasn't so lucky. She was working a flight to Raleigh around the holidays. A middle-aged, slightly overweight man was snoring loudly. At first it was kind of funny, but then his snoring became a nuisance. Passengers looked at him, clearly annoyed, thinking someone should shut him up. A short while later he stopped snoring. My friend said she thought he was sleeping so soundly, she didn't want to wake him up for the service. As everyone was deplaning, a man came up to the number one flight attendant and stated, "I think there is a dead person back there." This was such a simple statement for something so profoundly sad. The man sitting behind him was a doctor. He said he should have known something was wrong because his snoring was so abnormal. Along with his carry on, Christmas presents were found in the overhead bin.

Apparently the presents were for his family, who were eagerly waiting for him at the gate in the airport.

That event flashed through my mind as I was working as a coach galley flight attendant on an international flight bound for Guatemala. I noticed a tiny, elderly Guatemalan man coming down the aisle. He had a concerned look on his face and his color did not look right. As he approached me, his dark eyes rolled back in his head. I caught him before he fell to the floor. *Oh no, not on my flight.* I dragged him to the exit row seat where there was more room. My training flashed thru my mind. I thought for sure I was going to have to perform CPR.

Just as I was about to get help, his eyes opened. A tiny smile appeared on his little round face. With the language barrier, I asked a Spanish speaking passenger to translate. He hadn't eaten and felt faint and passed out. We gave him some fluids and food. Thankfully he was fine.

23

Rio de Janeiro

*O*ne of my favorite international layovers, as you know, was Rio de Janeiro. Most of the crew wanted to go out and do something fun because there is so much to explore.

On one particular layover, three of us decided to take the cable car to Mount Christo to see the Christ the Redeemer statue (the monument of Jesus standing with his arms spread out). When we arrived at the top of the mountain, we saw a church service taking place. The sermon was in Portuguese, but we thought it would be interesting to attend. We were so tired that the chairs looked very appealing.

The only seats available were in the middle section, so we had to climb over people to sit down. We got some unwelcome looks as we took our seats. As I was gazing in awe at the Christ statue, a freakishly large grasshopper with what had to be a two foot wing span landed on my arm. He grabbed me tightly, and I instinctively let out a loud scream. He flew off my arm and landed on top of a poor woman's head. She screamed even louder than I did. The preacher stopped his sermon to see what was causing all the commotion. Every eye in the place was fixed on us. As I sat frozen with embarrassment, he coolly surmised that the situation was not life threatening and calmly resumed his service. I will never forget that grasshopper.

On another Rio trip, I was flying with Karen, who had never been to Brazil. She wanted to go with me to the flea market that was located near Copa Cabana. I told her for safety reasons she should not bring her camera or purse. I also advised her to stuff money in different pockets so should we get robbed, we would lose only what is in the one pocket.

After changing our clothes, we met downstairs in the lobby. The first thing I noticed was a purse dangling off Karen's shoulder. *Oh well, I warned her!* Our plan was to take the bus over and walk back. It was probably a twenty minute walk.

The flea market is full of vendors who set their tents up to sell their wares. They have unbelievably low prices, which I took advantage of to stock up on Christmas presents. In the midst of our shopping spree, a young Portuguese man stopped Karen and me and asked for money. He must have been 16 or 17 years old. We told him politely no and continued walking around. After shopping exhaustion set in, we decided it was time to return to the hotel.

As we were walking, I felt someone might be following us. I instructed Karen to continue walking and keep talking. I pretended pointing to something of interest to get a glimpse at who it was behind us. Sure enough, it was the kid who asked us for money earlier. I told Karen I thought he was about to try something and warned her to be prepared.

The main street was ahead of us. We crossed the alley to see if he was following us. He indeed was and made his move.

"Give me your money," he said in broken English.

"No mas dinero," I said.

He grabbed Karen's purse that was dangling from her shoulder. She yanked it back and shouted, "No!" He looked at us stunned and then ran off.

Later on I reflected on just how lucky we had been. He could have had a knife or a gun.

24

Survivors

$\mathscr{F}$ear of flying can be totally debilitating for some people. I'm not sure if it's a control issue or simply a fear of crashing. Whatever it is, it's real.

Through the years, I've met survivors of airplane crashes who shared their amazing stories with me. It is astonishing that despite a fear of crashing, they get back on an airplane and fly again. The following excerpts are some of the stories survivors have shared with me.

In 1990, an Avianca airplane ran out of fuel. It crashed just before landing in New York. Two weeks later, I met a male passenger who was on that flight. He came on board with crutches and had bandages all over him. His right ear was gone. I asked how in the world he could possibly fly again. He said he was sleeping when they crashed. He woke up in a helicopter, which was taking him and another passenger to the hospital. That's when he found out about the crash. Because he had no memory of it, he was still able to fly.

A United airplane lost all hydraulics on its aircraft. The captain and first officer did a miraculous job landing the airplane. Unfortunately on impact, the airplane crashed and cartwheeled into a corn field in Iowa. I met a male passenger who had been on that flight. He said he was sitting in the rear section of the airplane. He asked the agent before they took off if he could switch seats further up and moved. His original row was where the majority of the passengers were killed and had he remained there, he would not have survived.

Another passenger told the story of how his plane crashed in Little Rock, Arkansas. He was sitting in first class and survived, while a young woman in the same row did not make it. After the airplane crashed and stopped moving, he asked the flight attendant who was strapped in her jumpseat if she was okay. She tried to get up but couldn't. Looking down he noticed her feet were facing the wrong direction. He carried her out to safety. It was pitch black outside with the rain pounding on his face while he waded in swampy water. I asked how he could get on an airplane again. He said he doesn't travel on Tuesdays and that it is therapeutic to talk about the experience.

An Alaskan airplane had a problem with its horizontal stabilizer. This equipment must be in working order to land the airplane. The captain knew the severity of the situation and decided to circle above the ocean instead of circling over land while trying to troubleshoot. They eventually crashed into the ocean and everyone perished. A month later, I met a young man on my flight. He stopped me in the aisle. "Hey look," he said, as he showed me a cover of TIME magazine with his face on it. His parents were on the Alaskan Airlines airplane that went down. They were missionaries helping to construct several buildings in Mexico. He and his wife had adopted his parent's commitment to helping others. I asked how he was doing. "I'm okay, but my younger sister is having a hard time."

My mom and I were flying from Atlanta to Raleigh. It was very foggy upon landing. As we were driving out of the airport parking lot, we noticed police cars, ambulances, and fire engines racing around. "Mom, something really terrible has happened here," I said. We quickly drove home and turned on the television. A special bulletin came on the screen. An American Eagle plane had crashed in Raleigh. There were no survivors.

25

I'll Take It on the Side

$\mathscr{I}$ looked forward to flying my trip from Miami to Paris. Two flight attendants work the business class section of a 767 aircraft. I was working the left aisle attending to fourteen passengers for the eight hour flight.

When passengers board the airplane, I instinctively check them out and get a feel for their personality. A stylish woman with long, straight, blonde hair, dressed like the latest cover of Vogue walked onto the airplane. She dropped her name brand suitcase in the aisle and waited. A man behind her stood for a moment and then dutifully picked up her luggage and placed it in the overhead bin. She sat in the first row of business class on my side. The chivalrous gentleman proceeded to coach. Wow, so much for assumptions. I mistakenly thought the male passenger was her well-trained husband.

I offered champagne and orange juice for the pre-departure service. When I reached the first row, the lady interrupted my service and barked, "Take this coat." *How rude,* I thought. She could have cared less that I was carrying a silver tray full of beverages. I told her I would hang her jacket when I was finished doing pre-departures. She threw me a look of icy displeasure. A few minutes later, I offered her some orange juice or champagne. "I'll take a club soda with lime easy on the ice," she snapped. *Looks like I have a real winner here.* I dubbed her the "Ice Princess".

The flight attendants like to gather around and talk about what's going on and who's causing trouble. It's therapy to get it out of our system. I shared how horrible this person was with the business class galley flight attendant, Kathy.

The unfriendly passenger wore a stunning fur-lined suit. I am sure she was someone special in life, or thought she was, but usually the truly wealthy people are down to earth. In fact, a lot of the time we can tell who is sitting in first class on a full fare ticket and who is an upgrade by the way they act. It is almost as though the upgraded passengers think if they are rude and arrogant, it will prove they are worthy to sit up there. I handed out menus to everyone.

After we took off, I asked for her dinner preference. I knew what was ahead. "How is the fish prepared? Is the chicken breaded? Does the pasta have any meat in it?" *Oh brother, how am I supposed to know?* Airplane food comes frozen, with tin foil placed on top of an oven-safe dish. Our job is to heat it up. The menu explained in detail how it was prepared and listed the ingredients. I tried to appease her and was as helpful as I could be, but nothing I said seemed to meet with her approval. After completing the preferences for the rest of the cabin, I shared with Kathy the on-going misfortune of placating this difficult passenger.

We prepare everything from a cart for our food service. The business class aisle flight attendants work alone on the cart while the galley flight attendant checks on us from time to time to see if we need anything. To look more professional, we wear a black-and-white checked serving jacket, which has two pockets on the front.

Our first course is an appetizer. It usually consists of shrimp cocktail, salmon and cream cheese, or prosciutto and melon. We serve a salad that comes with a choice of dressing (usually creamy peppercorn or vinaigrette). The dressings are placed in the first drawer with ladles in a glass container. We always begin our service with the first row.

My first passenger, of course, was the Ice Princess. I asked her which dressing she would prefer. "I want the creamy peppercorn, on the side. I reached over and poured some water into her glass. What I didn't realize was when I leaned over, the dressing's ladle hooked onto my jacket pocket.

I leaned back and the ladle of dressing launched into the air; flinging the creamy dressing all over the first row. It was all over the window, the floor, and of course to my horror, all over the Ice Princess' fur lined suit.

Both our mouths gaped open and she shot me a look that could kill. I looked up frantically trying to get Kathy's attention. She witnessed the whole thing and was doubled over with laughter.

In a panic, I pushed the cart back to the galley and ran to the restroom. I gathered some paper towels and rushed back to her. The paper towels smeared a white trail on her suit. When Kathy finally gained her composure, we found some linens and soaked them in our world famous remedy for stains: club soda.

Back I went to try and minimize the damage. She, as expected, didn't handle it gracefully. In fact, she was so upset, the entrée on which she had so carefully deliberated went uneaten!

The show had to go on and I delivered the rest of the passengers' trays. All of a sudden I was seized with a fit of uncontrollable laughter. I am not saying I am glad it happened, but sometimes life has its own way of balancing out. I gave the Ice Princess a cleaning voucher along with my apologies. A free bottle of red cabernet hopefully eased some of her lingering anguish.

26

Fuel Leak

$\mathscr{S}$mells on the airplane are just part of the job. The A-300 aircraft smells like a barn in the back. Flights from Seattle to Miami are a gas fest because the passengers are continuing on after a fourteen hour flight from Tokyo. And of course, we know we are in trouble when a passenger brings a newspaper or book into the lavatory. It all makes for a pretty stinky job sometimes. We have learned to take this in stride but every now and then our nose turns out to be our friend.

Those of you who have flown know when you are sitting on the runway, you may occasionally experience residual exhaust fumes from the planes ahead of you. That is normal. This following incident, however, was abnormal.

The captain always tells the flight attendants during the briefing: "You are the eyes and the ears of the aircraft. If there is anything unusual, let us know." In this case, we were the 'nose' of the aircraft.

We were on a Super-80, which holds 132 passengers. I was flight attendant number one flying from Orange County to Chicago (about a four-hour flight).

As I stepped into the aircraft that morning, I smelled a strong fuel odor. Making my way to the back of the aircraft, I noticed it was still there. It was like raw fuel, not fumes we smell from other aircrafts. I called the captain to come back and get his opinion. He said he smelled it but didn't think it was anything out of the ordinary. Over time it did seem to dissipate.

We boarded the airplane and took off. The flight was uneventful until we landed in Chicago. Quickly, the situation deteriorated.

In the middle of chatting with the flight attendant sitting next to me on the front jumpseat, I stopped the conversation.

"Do you smell something?"

"Yeah, I do" she said. I glanced in the cabin and saw the passengers reaching for their personal air control vents to get some fresh air.

I immediately called the captain and asked, "Do you smell anything up there?"

He said, "Yes, it's up here, too."

The pilots did not seem overly concerned so I resumed my casual conversation with my fellow flight attendant. This time we were interrupted by the chimes of flight attendant call buttons. I looked into the aisle and this time I saw gray, hazy smoke in the cabin.

I felt the flushing sensation of adrenalin surging through my body. I immediately went into emergency mode. Scared but calm, I grabbed my cockpit key, turned the lock and poked my head into the cockpit while sitting on the jumpseat.

"Captain," I said. "There is smoke in the cabin — what do you want to do?"

I looked ahead through the cockpit window and saw that we were no longer on an active taxiway and our arrival gate was only about 50 feet away. The captain decided since the smoke was not dense and there was no evidence of flames, to advance toward the gate and have a speedy deplaning.

The gate agent opened the forward door to allow the passengers to exit the aircraft. As passengers stepped out, many were holding their mouths and coughing. The first officer was obviously shaken. She accidentally left the PA button on and all passengers deplaning could hear, "You mean we are still smoking?" she asked ground personnel in a panicked voice.

I never saw passengers move so fast.

We had a fuel leak and the right engine was smoking. As the passengers were trying to get some air by turning on their vents, the smoke was filtering into the cabin. I do not think at the time we knew the severity of our situation. Our procedure for smoke in the cabin is to immediately evacuate the aircraft. The captain had to make a judgment call to either proceed to the gate or give the command to evacuate the aircraft where it was. Popping the slides in the middle of the airport with catering trucks, baggage carriers and fuel tankers would be extremely dangerous for passengers as well as ground personnel. On the other hand, a fuel leak could trigger a catastrophic explosion. I thought the pilots did an outstanding job and made the right decision.

Later the captain hugged me for the longest time. "Do you know how close that was?" he asked. We were very lucky to have landed when we did, had that fuel leak occurred mid-flight it could have been extremely dangerous with a vastly different outcome.

27

Prison Camp

$\mathcal{W}$e have a lot of time to share stories in the back of the aircraft and we often reminisce about our lives before we were flight attendants. It is another reason I enjoy flying so much. On one trip, the flight attendants were remembering how much fun they had during college. I was so envious when they spoke about their sororities, events they attended, and what degrees they earned. My college experience was not that great, but nonetheless, I do have a few stories to share about it.

My dad wanted one of his children to attend a Bible college. I was the youngest of five and none of my siblings had attended, so I was the "lucky" one. I had no aspirations of becoming a preacher; I already knew that I wanted to be a flight attendant, but not wanting to disappoint my father, I agreed to enroll.

It was a fairly new college campus at the time. There wasn't any grass; only a bunch of contemporary brick buildings scattered on clay soil. My mom and dad were reluctant to leave me there. It seemed so cold and uninviting.

The rooms were cramped yet large enough to hold two bunk beds. I was anxious to see who my roommates were going to be. We weren't allowed to have a TV in our room. All of us shared a single television located where the content could be strictly controlled and monitored.

My first roommate knocked on the door. I opened it to find one of the prettiest girls I had ever seen. Her name was Robin. She smiled timidly and walked in. We clicked and I liked her immediately! Later, our other roommate arrived. She was the complete opposite of Robin. She introduced herself and began reading her book. She wanted nothing to do with us, so I was glad Robin and I had each other.

Rules and regulations dictated our lives. We weren't allowed to go out on a date by ourselves: we either had to have a chaperone or double date. No public displays of affection such as holding hands were allowed and girls could only wear dresses to class. I often wondered why, because it seemed dresses were more flattering to the opposite sex than pants. But that was the rule.

I met a young man in one of my classes who happened to be the captain of the baseball team. He was very handsome with his deep, dark tan, and had a slight European accent. He asked me out on a date, but of course we had to have a chaperone. Luckily, a friend of mine met someone, so we were able to go on a double date (with permission that is)!

We had a great time getting away from the campus. At the end of the date, he kissed me so I kissed him back. Where I came from, kissing was no big deal. I guess here it was. The next day I heard rumors that I was easy because I kissed on the first date. *Oh brother. It was just a kiss.* Needless to say, that was it for him.

Robin and I were chosen to be on the pom-pom squad. The one thing that was missing from this school was some excitement and adventure, so we decided to make some of our own.

The boy's dormitory was right across from the girls. Our roommate was going to be out of town for the weekend, so we told some of the guys to look out their window around 9 p.m. "You'll see a show." We were desperate for some fun. I gave Robin a frilly outfit, and I put on another. They really weren't anything revealing; just some baby doll pajamas.

We turned on some music and did our little pom-pom routine for the guys across the way, enjoying their applause and appreciation. However, our giggles turned to anguish when someone knocked loudly on the door. We closed the shades, quickly changed into our pajamas, and slipped under the covers. The banging on the door continued.

I gingerly got up and opened the door while wiping my sleepy eyes.

"Yes," I said. It was the dean of men!

"I saw you girls from the other dorm," he said in his deep, commanding voice. "I am going to have to suspend you from all activities this weekend."

I explained it was very innocent; we were just having fun. He didn't want to hear any of it. If we were dancing erotically, I could understand, but it was only an innocent pom-pom routine.

The school required students take a minimum number of religious courses along with other academic studies. I was nearly overloaded with 21 credits. Among those were Christian Science, Theology, and Evangelism. Every day we had to attend chapel. We piled into a bus that took us to church. During that time, our room-mother would come by to check to see if our rooms were tidy. If they weren't perfect, we would receive a note saying specifically why it wasn't. If it passed inspection, the note simply said "great job" with a smiley face on it.

With all the homework and studying to do, chapel became a nuisance for Robin and me. I don't know which one of us came up with our next brainy scheme, but it was probably me. We had a drop ceiling in our room made of large, square pieces of tile that could be moved. We thought if we moved one of the large squares to the side, we could crawl up into the ceiling, take our flashlights with us, and do some studying during chapel.

That is exactly what we did. When it was time for chapel, we jumped on top of our bunk bed, crawled through the hole and sat on top of a steel support beam. We stayed there studying with our flashlights until we heard our room-mother come in and leave. This worked great for a couple of times. Unfortunately, as our room-mother was checking for tidiness, she saw there were remnants of ceiling chalk on the top of the bunk bed.

All of a sudden there was a loud knock underneath us. Our room-mother was thumping the ceiling with the hard end of a broomstick. Our hearts were beating harder than the broom. We were busted again. Humbly, we climbed down from the ceiling. Our room-mother vocalized how disappointed she was and sent us to the dean of women.

Each one of us took turns in the interrogation process. Robin went first. She left sobbing. *This couldn't be good.* The dean looked at me with coldness and without a word I followed her in. I explained how innocent it was and we were only studying.

"I swear to God that is all it was," I said.

"You swear?" she barked. "You are never to use the Lord's name in vain."

But I wasn't taking the Lord's name in vain. It was of no use. I had to sit there and listen to her lecture. The result was once again suspension for the weekend with no activities or television.

This school was getting old, really fast. I ran track in high school, so I thought I might try running. Maybe that would keep me out of trouble. At this point though, I wanted out. This was no place for me. I got so desperate I prayed, *"Please God, get me out of here."*

A miracle did happen that day. I was running around the track when my side began to hurt. I remember sitting next to a tree in terrible pain and sobbing. Not one person stopped to ask what was wrong. Not that I wanted them to either. I ate dinner and still felt the pain on the lower side of my abdomen. I walked up some steps and collapsed. An ambulance rushed me to the hospital.

The doctor said my white blood cell count was extremely high and that my appendix needed to come out. He called my parents and said he needed to operate immediately.

One thing I do believe in, is the power of prayer. I can't tell you how many times in my life where I prayed from the depths of my soul and my prayers were answered. My prayer to get me out of that school was no exception. After a week of healing from a successful appendectomy, I packed my things and never went back. *Hallelujah*!

28

Commuter Nightmare

I loved living in Atlanta! The seasons are mild and spectacular, especially the spring and fall with lingering color that lasts for several months. The negative part of living there was the traffic and commuting to work.

I always took the first flight of the day knowing that it usually goes out on time, which meant getting up at 2:30 AM. I gave myself plenty of time to get to the airport in the event of an accident. Once there, I parked my car, took an employee van, went through security — and waited an hour or more before my flight departed. It then took another hour and a half to fly to Miami. After arriving, I typically waited three to five hours before I actually began my shift. Sometimes I waited even longer. That first day is a killer. I ended up on my feet an average of seventeen to twenty three hours. But, it was my choice to live in a city where there is no base, so I couldn't complain about commuting.

One day I made my way to the Atlanta airport for the usual commute to Miami. The agent called out the group numbers to board. Passengers who awoke for these early morning flights boarded like zombies. I, too, stumbled onto the airplane in a sleepy daze. The beginning of the flight was uneventful. The passenger load was three quarters full. I was sitting in the exit row dressed in my uniform.

En route to Miami, I kept having a strange feeling I couldn't shake; a feeling of uneasiness best describes it. I looked out the window on our descent. I always enjoy seeing Tampa and the beautiful Gulf of Mexico as our flight path takes us over the west coast of Florida. Following the waterways, the airplane veers to the left and goes directly over the Everglades to Miami International Airport. The clear blue sky was dotted with just a few white puffy clouds.

About the time the wheels should have touched the runway, the plane took off again. I looked around alarmed. No one else seemed to think anything was wrong, but I couldn't shake that feeling. A few minutes later the captain announced, "Ladies and gentlemen, our cockpit indicator light shows that our nose gear is not locked. We are going to do a fly-by for the control tower to see if the gear is indeed down."

Ding Ding Ding! *I know what that sound is.* The pilots are communicating to the flight attendants that something is wrong and to prepare the cabin in case of an evacuation.

Soon, the flight attendants were in the aisles demonstrating the brace positions. Cross your hands in front of you and place your head on the seat, or grab the back of your ankles and place your head on your knees.

I knew they didn't have much time so being in uniform and sitting in the exit row, I got up and briefed the passengers also sitting in the exit rows on how to open the window exits in case of an emergency. I explained that if fire, smoke or debris is spotted, they should not open the window and instead evacuate to the nearest available exit. Most of the passengers looked at me as if I were kidding. "This is the real deal," I affirmed. "Be prepared to open these exits." They shook their heads in disbelief but understood.

The captain came on the PA, "Uh, ladies and gentlemen, the control tower said they see our landing gear is down, but they cannot tell if is locked. We are getting back in line. Flight attendants, prepare for landing."

Another couple of minutes went by with my heart beating wildly; my hands now drenched in sweat. In an unbelievably calm voice the captain said, "Ladies and gentlemen, we have thirty seconds upon landing, please assume your brace position." Everyone obediently placed their crossed hands on the seat in front of them. I was amazed at the silence. *This can't be happening. We have a 50/50 situation here.* I said a quick prayer.

Glancing out the window, I saw fire engines, police cars, and emergency trucks waiting for us. *Please don't collapse or cartwheel.*

Thud! We made it. Talk about an adrenalin rush. I was exhausted. However, I still had to continue on with the day and work my first flight.

And what can I get you to drink today?

29

Gotcha

$\mathscr{E}$veryone likes a good practical joke — especially if it is not played on them! Airline crews are notorious pranksters. The more memorable incidents were often aimed at new hires on their first day of work.

My initiation took me by surprise. Three good natured pilots snatched me up and stuffed me in the overhead bin! I learned later that it was a pretty common practice. I still distinctly remember being in there and all of us enjoying the prank. Those were the days!

A friend of mine shared her experience on her first trip. At the end of the flight, the captain called the flight attendants to let them know they had been selected for a random drug test. All crewmembers were to have a urine sample ready upon landing. Everyone in the crew was in on it but her. They each poured some apple juice in a glass and taped their name on the outside. They told Laura it was standard procedure. She took the empty glass and stepped into the lavatory. While in there, she thought to herself, "I am not going to do this." She opened the door and all the crewmembers toasted and gulped down their apple juice!

A particularly memorable captain's preflight briefing included information that catering may not have provided enough ice for the flight, so the new hire was instructed to count each ice cube before the gate agent closed the door. Another notable and harmless haze was to tell the newbies they needed to grab a barf bag and collect an air sample from the back of the aircraft for quality control!

On one of my flights, we had a brand new flight engineer. I called the cockpit during the flight to say we had a very unusual air leak. I told them we needed someone to come and check it out. I'm sure the captain knew what was going on and sent the flight engineer back to the cabin. Previously, I gave a few passengers pillows with instructions to throw them when I gave the signal. When the flight engineer walked to the aft galley, I told him the air leak went away. When he returned to the cockpit, I made a PA to welcome our flight engineer on his very first trip. As he walked through the aisle, everyone applauded and threw pillows at him.

There have been pantyhose sticking out of the pilots' suitcase as they rolled it through the airport, lipstick kisses on their bright white shirts, toilet papering their room overnight as they slept, and God only knows what else. As long as no one is hurt in the process, I'm all for making their first flight one they will not forget.

Sometimes the ramp personnel would get in on the action. When I was based in Dallas, our operations area was underneath the airport, also known as the dungeon. It was dreary down there. We also shared the area with other employees of the company. The ramp guys knew that the crewmembers were known to be a little on the cheap side, so they placed a nickel on the ground and glued it to the floor. It was strategically placed right in front of their operations area. They would laugh at all the pilots and flight attendants who bent over to pick up the nickel. Of course, being a starving new hire, I too fell for the old nickel-glued-to-the-floor trick!

My all-time favorite prank took place when I was based in Raleigh. I had been flying with the same crew the whole month, so we established a bond. I had gone to a novelty shop and found an unbelievably realistic pile of poop.

The first leg of our flight was a 5 a.m. sign-in. It was dark outside and dark on the airplane. I was first to enter the aircraft and quickly threw the poop prop on the floor of the galley. When the first officer turned the power on to the aircraft, the lights came on in the cabin. I screamed while pointing to the brown spiral of doo-doo. Other crewmembers screeched in horror. The pilots raced out of the cockpit to see what all the commotion was about. They muttered a few nasty comments about the caterers and decided to call cabin service to clean up the mess. I told them to never mind; I would take care of it. I grabbed a paper towel and squeamishly picked up the plastic pile and tossed it at one of the pilots! He jumped back trying to avoid the poop and once it hit the floor we all enjoyed the stunt together.

I flew international for many years out of Miami. I loved flying international but clearing Customs and Immigration was always a hassle. In Miami, the Customs' guys were shameless flirts. They would pull you aside under the guise of searching your bags just to start a conversation. It was harmless and kind of flattering at first, but when you are in a hurry to make your flight home, it wasn't fun anymore.

I was in my hotel room with my creative juices flowing trying to figure out how I could stop them from doing this. So, on one of my trips, I took a hair brush out of my bag and pulled all the hair from it, forming a hairball. When I arrived in Miami, sure enough the same Customs guy searched my bag. As he opened it, the wadded up hairball sprung out at him. He quickly closed my bag without saying a word. I was cracking up on the inside as he ushered me along.

After this worked, I decided I would try something else, so I took a tampon and again placed it on top of my clothes. I was targeted, as usual, for a bag search. This time he was thoroughly embarrassed and again quickly closed the suitcase and sent me on my way. I don't know if they talked about it among themselves; all I know is the searching and flirting came to an end.

30

AM or PM

$\mathscr{H}$ave you ever awakened from a nap and felt a little disoriented? A flight attendant whom I was flying with went way beyond a little disoriented.

It was an early sign-in for our trip. We ended up in Philadelphia, but it took three flights to get there. We arrived at 3:30 p.m. absolutely depleted. A nap was definitely needed for the three of us flight attendants.

Our number one flight attendant, Julie, said she wanted to sleep soundly, so she took her phone off the hook, put on her eye mask and drifted off to sleep.

Our van pickup for the morning was scheduled for 6:20 a.m. This poor girl woke up from a deep sleep; her alarm clock read 6:25. Seeing it was dark outside, she was sent into a horrible panic. Julie thought she was late for pickup. The phone was off the hook, so she assumed everyone had tried to wake her and went on ahead to the airport.

Immediately, she called the front desk and asked them to hail a cab. Knowing she had no time for a shower, Julie threw on her uniform, shoved everything into her bag and off she went to the airport in her cab.

Julie went through security and ran to the end of the terminal. Ironically, the Chicago evening flight was leaving around the same time we were the next morning. She ran down the jet bridge and threw her bags near the front closet informing the number one flight attendant she could go home now (thinking she was a reserve flight attendant who had been called in to replace her). The number one flight attendant didn't know what to say. "This is my flight," she insisted. Julie looked in the back of the aircraft and realized the flight attendants did not look familiar.

Embarrassed and confused, she slowly walked up the jet bridge to the gate. As Julie was pulling up her schedule on the computer, the agent hovered over her shoulder. He took a glance at her schedule and noticed the date.

"Oh honey," he said. "You need to go to the hotel. This is PM not AM."

31

Missing Flight Attendant

$\mathscr{A}$ll of the passengers were boarded and the flight attendants impatiently waited for our cockpit crew to arrive.

Finally, I saw them coming down the jet bridge. I recognized the captain.

"Norm, where have you been?" I jokingly asked. He had a blank expression on his face. "What's wrong?"

"I'll tell you later," he mumbled.

We did our beverage service. I was dying to know what happened, so I moseyed into the cockpit. Norman said the night before they had been on a Jamaica layover. There was an eclipse, so he and two flight attendants, Sally and Sandy, decided to hang out by the pool and view the sun and moon coming together. He was getting a little tired and decided to turn in. Sandy agreed she also was ready to go to bed, so she left with Norm. Sally said there was a handsome guy sitting across the pool. She wanted to hang out and see if anything might develop.

After about thirty minutes, Sandy felt guilty about leaving Sally alone, so she returned to keep her company. When she arrived at the pool, there was no one around. She assumed she must have gone back to her room to sleep.

The next morning there was no sign of Sally. She didn't show up for the shuttle to the airport. The security guard checked her room. Her suitcase was there, but her bed had not been slept in. The flight crew was desperate to find her. They didn't know what to do. Norm called the chief of pilots who suggested they continue on without her. The company would take over and try to locate Sally. Reluctantly, the crew boarded the shuttle van and left.

Thankfully, she was found. From what I understand, someone slipped the drug Rufinol into her drink and she had to be briefly hospitalized. I saw her several months later. She said she was okay but didn't want to talk about it. I thought of my own experience in Palm Beach.

There are a lot of scary people out there.

32

Rags to Riches

It took me about three years to start thinking about dating anyone seriously after Craig.

I was working first class on a flight from Miami to Aruba. As we were boarding, I heard what sounded like a huge party going on in first class. I glanced into the cabin. It seemed as though all the male passengers knew each other and were already having a good time. *I secretly wondered what I was in for.*

With passengers still boarding, I asked row by row if the party animals wanted something to drink. To my amazement, their manners and personalities were impressive. You could tell they were successful yet remained humble. Some of the more outgoing guys told me there was a mix-up at the ticket counter and explained that one of the men in their group ended up in coach instead of first class. They asked if I would go to the person sitting in 8D and make him feel at home. They were all nice guys, so I had no problem with that.

I walked back to row eight. When I made eye contact with him, I noticed he had piercing blue eyes. They twinkled when he smiled. He was a little older than me. I was in my early-30s and he was in his mid-40s. I could tell by looking at him that he was a good person.

Before we took off, the agent discovered the mix-up in the first class section and that Tom (Mr. 8D) should be sitting there instead of another passenger, so they switched seats.

I had a great time throughout the flight with the guys. All were successful businessmen, doctors, lawyers, etc., but you would never know it. They were down to earth, fun guys to be around.

I needed to rest for a while, so I secluded myself in the galley by closing the curtain. After a short time, Tom came in. He seemed so genuine, clearly someone who felt comfortable in his own skin. We talked for a while. I asked if he was married and he said no.

After the flight was over, all twelve passengers asked if our crew would like to meet up with them later that night in Aruba. This would be a very long day for us. I explained we still had to fly to San Juan then back to Aruba and wouldn't be getting in until midnight. I told Tom to give me a call at the hotel and I would let him know if we were interested.

It was near midnight when I walked into the hotel room, barely having the energy to wash my face. While taking off my mascara, the phone rang.

"Hey, can we send over a limo and pick you up?" Tom asked.

I apologized to him, "No thank you though, we are all just too tired." One of his friends got on the phone. He did his best to make his case, talking about Leer jets and emphasizing how crazy this guy was about me.

In spite of the hard sell, I politely declined, but shared I would be sunbathing by the pool the next day around 10 a.m.

I thought that was that and presumed I would never see Tom again. I knew from the flight the guys had a scheduled golf tee time in the morning. I sipped my delicious coffee on the balcony while watching the glorious sunrise.

Wasting no time, I threw on my bikini, put my hair up and dashed out to the pool to catch some rays. I really didn't think Tom would show up, but as I rotated my body for maximum sun exposure there he was coming toward me. He said good morning and asked if I wanted to go for a walk with him on the beach.

We talked along the white sandy shore for about three hours. I told Tom my story about Craig. He shared his story of his 8-year-old daughter who had a life threatening illness where recovery did not look promising. It was very sad. I asked where her mother was. He said they were separated but not legally divorced. They didn't want their daughter's days to be marred by a messy divorce. I understood, but a red flag was waving back and forth.

"Listen," I said. "I would never have an affair with a married man. If this is anything but what you say it is, it's on your shoulders."

He swept me off my feet. For the next eight months, I went on an unbelievable journey of love, excitement, and the time of my life. Money can't make you happy, but you sure can have a lot of fun with it!

One of the hardest things about meeting someone on the airplane is distance — he usually doesn't reside anywhere close by. Tom was no exception. Our first conversation on the phone was very comfortable. He asked me about my dreams, hopes and regrets. He owned his own company and was a financial planner. Tom said the smartest thing you can do as far as running a company is to treat your employees well. He told me he pays them well, and that in return they have given him years of complete loyalty. I loved his integrity.

For our first date, Tom wanted to surprise me. He wouldn't tell me where we were going, only that I was to bring a nice dress. I thought maybe he was going to take me to Florida, so I purchased a beautiful cream-colored dress with lace capped sleeves and the jewelry, pantyhose and shoes to match. I didn't have a lot of money, so this was extravagant for me.

Tom called a few hours before his plane took off for Atlanta. He hinted something about New York tomorrow night. *Oh no*, I thought. "A cream-colored dress will never do; I need a black one." I took off for the mall again. I bought the black dress along with all the accessories. He was worth it, I rationalized.

I was a little disappointed that Tom didn't fly his Leer jet, but hey, commercial airlines aren't that bad. We arrived in New York and took a cab to Manhattan. We stayed at a hotel overlooking Central Park. I felt like a princess! I made it clear there would be no romantic involvement. He was a perfect gentleman.

One of my dreams we had discussed earlier on the phone was to see the play "Phantom of the Opera." Tom had the perfect evening planned: the Rainbow Room and a play afterward. I was in heaven! It was like God had given me the worst in my first marriage, and now he gave me the very best in this relationship. The play was fabulous, and the "Phantom of the

Opera" was now our theme song. Magically, we heard it everywhere we went.

Our next date took us to Florida. This time I had the dress ready to go. We stayed in a fabulous hotel on the ocean. I walked into the room and there were two dozen roses waiting. Tom had a basketball perched on a vase because earlier I told him I could beat the pants off of him in a game of HORSE. He was attentive, thoughtful and had a great sense of humor.

Next, Tom came to Atlanta where it was my turn to show him the sights. I took him to the Blue Ridge Mountains where we explored the many waterfalls and small towns. We had a blast!

Chicago was our next adventure. We stayed in a hotel that had a spiral staircase in our room. We took the little boat tour that meandered throughout the city. On this day, there was a slight breeze with the smell of chocolate wafting in the air. It was truly delightful! I fell pretty hard for him.

For our next adventure, I found myself on a boat soaking up the sun in Lake Tahoe. It was just the two of us. We rented a house off the lake with a spectacular view from every room. Later that evening, we decided to see Diana Ross in concert. We didn't have any tickets, but he didn't seem too concerned.

When we arrived at the concert, Tom stuffed some money in the attendant's hand. He escorted us to the very front table right in front of Diana. We were so close to her I could reach out and touch her dress. *What a world! I could get used to this.*

We had very special times together, but our next and final adventure led us to California. First, we stayed in downtown San Francisco. We took a ride in a helicopter. I can't remember if we flew over or under the San Francisco Bay Bridge. All I know is, that it was spectacular!

We rented a car and drove down U.S. 1 to Pebble Beach, staying at the famous Pebble Beach Lodge and eating an extravagant meal. We retired to our cozy room, lying there in front of the crackling fire.

When I returned home, it was a couple of days before I heard from him. I thought this was highly unusual because he previously had been calling every day. Tom finally called.

"Is there something wrong?" I asked.

Indeed there was. Someone who knew Tom and his wife had seen us together at Pebble Beach. They had called his estranged wife and shared they had seen Tom and I together. He said he should have told her earlier, but his main concern was for his daughter. He said his daughter asked all about me.

"Why do you like her?" she asked.

"Because she smiles just like you," he told her.

"Does she know how to swim?" she questioned. "Are you moving to Atlanta?"

He thought it would be okay and was relieved that everything was out in the open.

From what I understood, the next morning his little girl wouldn't wake up. She was rushed to the hospital. Apparently she left a note saying something to the effect of "I can't live life without my Daddy." She had taken lots of medicine and had to have her stomach pumped. I felt sick. Tom was totally despondent. I recommended he take her to see a psychologist. I also told him I could not be indirectly responsible for someone else's life again. Please don't call me until your divorce is final, I advised. I wished him the best.

He called a couple of weeks later to inform me he was taking his daughter to a therapist and everything was fine. I received a dozen roses for Christmas and for Valentine's Day the following year. It was an amazing time, but it was over.

33

The Young and the Lifeless

I love babies! I love the way they smell (most of the time). I love their look of curiosity. I love the way they feel when you hold them. Needless to say, every time I have a chance to cuddle with one on the airplane, I take advantage of the opportunity.

The only thing the flight attendants think of on the last leg of a three-day trip is going home. We don't want any mechanical issues, weather delays or medical emergencies. We just want to go home.

As we were boarding our last flight of the trip, I noticed a little bundle of joy dressed in her Sunday best. She held out her little hand to me as she passed by. *Oh good, I found someone to hold and cuddle.*

After we completed our beverage service, a flight attendant call light came on. A female passenger asked me for some juice. She informed me when she awakened from her nap, she felt a little light-headed. I asked if she was on any medication. She said no. I made sure her seat was fully reclined, put a direct air flow on her from the vent and told her to take off her jacket. I went to the galley and told the other flight attendant what was going on. "Oh great, just when we are going home," she said. *My sentiments exactly.*

I gathered ice in a cloth and poured juice to give to the passenger. I instructed her to place the cloth on her forehead for a few minutes then rotate it to the back of her neck. If she needed anything at all, I instructed her to ring the flight attendant call button.

As I was walking toward the rear of the airplane, I spotted the little bundle of joy I noticed in the boarding process.

"Do you mind if I hold your baby for a while?" I asked her mother. Moms usually enjoy the break.

"She probably won't go to you, but you can try."

I flashed a big smile at the baby and out flung her arms. She looked eager for a new friend. I reached for the little bundle and walked the cutie to the front of the aircraft. Whenever I hold a baby, they instinctively look into my eyes to see if they can trust me. Once trust has been established, they feel comfortable going with me. All of the passengers were cooing at her as we walked by them in the aisle.

The coffeemakers have small colored lights on them that flash when we turn them on and off. Babies are mesmerized by them, including little Emma. After we played lights for a while in the first class galley, I walked into the main cabin to return Emma to her mom. Before I reached her row the call light went on again. This time the passenger next to the ill passenger rang it.

"I think she passed out," the adjacent passenger said in alarm. I handed little Emma back to her mom and quickly explained, "I have an emergency."

I ran up to the number one flight attendant and told her I was getting oxygen for a passenger. She notified the captain.

I walked through the cabin not holding a precious bundle of joy, but a cold tank of oxygen. The passengers were gasping instead of cooing. I sat next to the now semi-conscious and confused passenger. This was my first time using the oxygen in an emergency situation. I didn't realize how tough the plastic that wrapped the mask was to open. My adrenalin was kicking in as my hands began to tremble. I got the mask out and put it on her nose and mouth.

Years back, I had flown with a flight attendant who recounted a story of her oxygen tank exploding when turned on. She showed me the scars on her hands and arms. She was fired for being unsightly, but she later got her job back. That was a long time ago. Now it was my turn to turn on the oxygen. Her story was now in the back of my mind.

Slowly, I turned the knob. "Don't be left without oxygen" is our reminder to turn the knob to the left. I closed my eyes and heard the whooshing noise of the oxygen turning on. Thank God it didn't explode!

A male passenger who saw what was going on asked his wife, who was a medical doctor, if she would be willing to assist. She volunteered her services and basically took over from there asking for a stethoscope.

I later checked on the passenger. Her clammy, pale skin had now returned to a healthy, pinkish hue. She apologized profusely and felt embarrassed by the whole incident. I shared with her the same thing happened to my mom. She had been very active the day she was returning home from her trip. On the flight, she got up to use the restroom. She started to see stars and fell into the lavatory door. The flight attendant administered oxygen and she was fine.

We deplaned without further incident, I shared a caring goodbye with the recovered passenger and a warm smile with little baby Emma.

I acted as though it was just another flight but the truth was it took a lot out of me. I was exhausted when I got home.

34

The Second Time Around

$\mathscr{F}$our years and many flights had passed since my disastrous marriage. I reached a point in my life where I wanted to settle down. My wall was coming down, but my antenna was still up. I kept watching for warning signs with each guy whom I dated.

I had a list of qualities and values I was looking for in a potential husband. I don't mean a list in my head; I literally wrote down my wish list of qualities with columns next to them. I didn't want to make any mistakes, so every date I had, I would go home and check off the qualities he possessed. Those poor guys! I am a bit ashamed of how hard I was. Most of them lasted only a few dates. After all, I was 32 years old and thought I didn't have much time to waste!

Finally, on a flight to London it happened: I met my husband! The flight attendants I was working with were the matchmakers.

Before the flight took off on a MD-11 aircraft, some of the more senior flight attendants asked why I wasn't married yet. I told them I was just looking for a nice guy. I didn't care if he was the most handsome man in the world. I just wanted a nice guy. Of course, I didn't tell them about my checklist. By the way, some of the things on my list weren't impossible to fulfill. A belief in God was important to me. He should love to watch a beautiful sunrise and sunset. I wanted someone who opened the door for me. I was still an old-fashioned girl who believes in chivalry and good manners. I was tired of commuting, so I also wished my future husband might live in Florida.

I was the business class galley flight attendant on that flight. I had two flight attendants with me who delivered the service. It was hard work with a full load of fifty six passengers who sat in the business class section. The seat configuration was two seats on the sides and five seats in the middle. AB-CDEFG-HJ. There were two aisles in which each flight attendant worked parallel sides.

Halfway through the service, both flight attendants came rushing from the aisles. "Get me a chateaubriand and go look at this passenger, he's a nice guy!" I quickly threw some steak, potatoes and veggies on a plate and handed it to the flight attendant. Because he was sitting in an E seat — the very middle — there had been a mix up on who was to serve him. He was reading his newspaper when one of the flight attendants asked if he wanted any dessert. He casually said, "Actually, I haven't eaten my meal yet." That was when they scurried to the galley. He handled it gracefully without any fuss at all and clearly impressed the flight attendants.

Curiosity got the best of me and I ventured into the aisle to get a glimpse of the gracious passenger. He had big, blue eyes with long lashes and light brown hair with golden highlights from the sun. I had work to do, so I headed back to the galley.

After I finished cleaning up after the service, the forgotten passenger entered the galley where I was working. His back was hurting and asked if I would mind if he stood in the corner for a while. I actually thought it was kind of funny that he and I were so casual and relaxed around each other. I did not really flirt with him, however we did strike up a conversation and it evolved into something meaningful.

We talked for about forty-five minutes. I knew within the first twenty that he was going to be my husband. I wasn't nervous around him and could be myself. Was he perfect? No. Was I? Heck no!

I shared my feelings about old fashion values and roles in relationships. He was only a few years older than me and it was clear we shared similar values. Our casual conversation began to feel more intimate. I looked at him in the eye, a bit differently just then. I asked if he had tried the cookie ice cream we were serving. He hadn't, so I spoon fed him a bite of mine. Okay, I was flirting with him now!

Another passenger asked me for something, so I had to get busy. He went back to his seat. I had just finished reading a book called "The Rules." Basically, the book described how to snag a man. One of the rules was to never give a guy your number first. I waited for a long time for this passenger to make some kind of move, but he never did. I thought he was a very sensitive, kind person and you don't find guys like that every day, so I broke the golden rule. I wrote down my number and handed it to him. I enticed him by letting him know I had free buddy passes if he wanted to be my travel buddy. He said he had a boat and would love to have some companionship. We were definitely letting each other know that we were both single and available. So much for the rules!

We were engaged four months later and married within nine months. I had written down in my notebook I would like to be married within one year and move to Florida. We were and I moved from Atlanta to Delray Beach, Florida. Maybe there is something to be said for a wish list. I also know that in love sometimes your heart bends the rules. Daryl and I were married in 1996 and have been very happily married ever since.

35

Silicone Survivor

At the age of 13, I said to my mom, "All my friends are wearing a bra but me." She bought me one, a training bra, but there really wasn't anything to train. I went through high school wearing padded bras, but one incident really stood out where I wore a halter top with no bra. A boy said to me, "A half an egg is bigger than you." I laughed, but I was humiliated.

At 21, I decided I was tired of being flat chested. I had done a couple of beauty pageants, (one modeling a swimsuit) but I wanted to feel more feminine. I made an appointment with a female plastic surgeon, who agreed I could use some help. I was a double A cup. (For those men out there who don't know what that is, it's the smallest size you can be.) Because I was so thin, she recommended I only go up one size to a B cup. That was fine with me and we went ahead with the silicone implants. I had to keep the bandages on for six weeks. When I took them off, I couldn't believe it. Voila! Breasts! I loved them. Because they were only a B cup, they looked and felt completely natural.

I was married at the age of 33. Those implants had been in for twelve years by that time. (Studies now show that ten years may be the life expectancy of the implants.) When we were first married, I was very active. We used to take trips to New England for the fall season. As we were walking along the rapids, I said to Daryl, "Let's see who can hit that big rock over there first." We took turns taking pebbles and throwing them at our target. My throws traveled just as far as his and we enjoyed the mild competition. About two years later, we took that same trip and again played the target game. To my surprise my throws were weak and short, traveling only a few yards. My husband looked at me and said jokingly, "Hey you're throwing like a girl." My strength was zapped and I didn't know why.

I also felt unexplainably tired at times; I could barely lift my arm. Everything I did seemed like such an effort.

My scalp was always itching. I told the dermatologist it felt as if the itching were inside my head, but she didn't see anything abnormal. I was losing my hair. I asked my stylist, "Do you see anything that may be causing my hair to fall out by the root?" There was a visible white clump attached to some strands of hair that fell from my head. She saw nothing.

A rash appeared on the side of my face that wouldn't go away. The dermatologist gave me a glycolic peel and was alarmed at the reaction of the rash. It was bright red. She didn't recognize it and could not diagnose it.

One day I was trying on clothes. I pulled my shirt above my head and felt a horrible pain shoot down my back. I thought I must have pulled a muscle. The pain lingered. Lumps started to form on my shoulders and neck, first on the right side and then eventually migrating to the left. My husband joked that I looked a bit like a body builder. The lumps burned and were painful. I constantly massaged them trying to eliminate the bulges and pain.

Then, I began to experience problems swallowing my food. The episodes came sporadically. Food would get caught in my esophagus, causing awful pain. Drinking liquids during the episodes only made it worse. Once, while I was working first class it happened yet again. I was jumping up and down on one leg and pounding on my chest. I must have looked not only ridiculous but scary, because at that moment the captain came out of the cockpit to use the lavatory. He was so alarmed he asked if he should make an emergency landing. I said that would not be necessary and tried to force myself to regurgitate the lodged piece of food. Even if I did throw up the food, the pain continued for a short time. Only until everything had completely settled in my stomach would the pain and spasms go away. I went to a gastroenterologist. He did an endoscopy and to my surprise found nothing wrong.

The most tragic thing of all was losing the use of my hands. I was buttoning my blouse when a twinge of pain soared between my thumb and forefinger on my right hand. It felt as if I had split a tendon. I couldn't shake hands with anyone because the pain was so bad. I had to be careful putting on my flight attendant jumpseat harness because it would cause shooting pain down my arms and hands. I thought the pain eventually would go away, but it only transferred to my fingers and the back of my hand. It eventually migrated to my left hand. I was 36 years old at the time, but felt like I was 90.

I was making cookies and cupcakes for the Fourth of July and could barely frost them due to the intense pain. If I carried anything for a period of time, my hands would stay frozen in that position temporarily, causing more pain and muscle cramping. After hanging up the phone, my hand looked similar to a claw and they were always cold.

I knew flight attendants were known for getting carpal tunnel syndrome, which would explain the hand pain. I knew stress could cause lumps in your neck and shoulder area. I knew choking on your food could be a hereditary hiatal hernia. My burning and itching scalp could be a skin disorder, as well as my rash. I couldn't explain my loss of energy, though. Why was my strength zapped from me? I was still young. It got to the point where my neck would barely move to the left. I continued massaging and massaging, trying to ease the burning bulges. My family said they saw me fading away and there was nothing they could do about it. I looked like death.

On one particular flight after all the passengers had deplaned, I noticed a magazine on one of the seats. The headline read, "Are your implants making you sick?" I read the article with great enthusiasm and hope. It finally dawned on me. All of those women who won lawsuits for autoimmune disorders and other health issues related to implants were legitimate. I guess I had believed the doctors who said no correlation existed.

I immediately called the surgeon who was mentioned in the article. She suspected I was in the advanced stages and recommended immediate removal. I had the silicone implants in for sixteen years. I loved them as they were part of me. The thought of going back to an A cup wasn't too appealing, but my doctor said my body would need to heal before replacing them.

The surgery to remove the implants was a success. The silicone implants had indeed both ruptured — one of them grotesquely. All I had to do was gently squeeze the implant and silicone oozed out. Every time I laid down on my stomach, it seeped out and into my body. Each time someone gave me a hug, more and more leaked out. Once ruptured, almost every move I made advanced the symptoms. It was having a devastating effect on my body!

I have been asked several times if I noticed a change in my breast size or shape during those years. I had gained a little weight and everything seemed normal in appearance. I was told when silicone travels through your body, it has a hard time naturally being eliminated since it is a foreign substance. It is common to gravitate to the extremities causing a silicate to form. I immediately went on a detoxification regimen and strict diet to purge the toxins. I would say 85 percent of the pain is gone. My energy has returned and I am somewhat back to normal. Some lingering hand pain still occurs, but the lumps in my shoulders have diminished and I no longer experience searing pain up and down my nerves.

I share my story with everyone I can in case they may have or may know someone who has silicone implants. Of course, flight attendants are notorious for having implants. I received a call from one who remembered my story years ago. She experienced nearly identical symptoms and was electing to have her implants removed and wanted to know all about the procedure.

I have talked to a flight attendant about her scarred hand from surgery due to silicone poisoning. Another flight attendant showed me her bulging knuckles. And another said she has tumors located around her uterus due to her ruptured implants.

The surgeon who removed my implants said there have been many babies born with severe birth defects related to silicone poisoning. Maybe it was a blessing for me and my husband not to have had children.

My doctor asked if I would be willing to be part of a segment on Fox News about surviving silicone rupture and the risk of silicone poisoning. The segment was actually about the controversy of the new silicone implant. I showed my ruptured implant with the silicone oozing out on TV. It is a sticky substance that looks and feels like adhesive glue. It took me a while to scrub it off my hands. I showed a hairball from my brush where my hair would fall out from the root. Several people I knew saw the segment. Sure enough, a flight attendant called to talk about her implants. That made it all worthwhile.

I am not condemning implants by any means. I just want to make sure that if anyone else is experiencing unexplained health issues and has a history of implant surgery there may be a correlation and they should be aware. The girl who shared her story in that magazine article, I believe, saved my life. I hope I can help someone in a similar way.

36

Weapon of Mass Evacuation

After living in Florida for many years, my husband and I decided on a change of scenery and moved to Atlanta. That meant commuting to work again.

My upcoming 2-day trip was easily commutable. I would leave Atlanta on the early morning flight, fly my trip, and return the next day on the last flight — perfect, on paper. Unfortunately, it did not turn out that way.

We've all done some things we are not proud of. This particular instance was one of complete exasperation!

My flights were on schedule the first day. The second day, however, brought major weather delays. As a result, I was clearly going to miss my connection home to Atlanta. Needless to say, I was not a happy camper. This meant I would either pay the expense of a hotel room or stay in flight operations and sleep in a chair. Neither option was appealing.

The last leg of my trip was Chicago - Miami. It was bumpy all the way. After being tossed around while doing the beverage service, I couldn't wait to sit down for a break in the galley. Looking down at my watch, I saw it was getting close to 10:30 p.m. I usually go to bed around 9, so I was getting a little tired and grumpy.

I settled into my jumpseat enjoying a few minutes of much needed time to myself when three male passengers sporting their business polo shirts invaded my galley. At this point, I didn't want to talk to anyone, so I opened a magazine and buried my nose in it, hoping they would get the hint. I let them chat for a bit but they were getting on my nerves. Coincidentally, the seat belt sign flashed on, as the air turned choppy.

"Hey you guys," I said. "The seatbelt sign is on; you better go ahead and sit down."

"Yeah, yeah, yeah," they said in agreement, but never followed through.

The choppy air became more turbulent. "You need to sit down," I told them again. They laughed, thinking I wasn't being serious and ignored my request.

I was irritable, exhausted and my stomach was bloated from the huge bean burrito I had devoured in Chicago. I did something I had never done before. I passed a lethal SBD (silent, but deadly) blast of gas! The odor was just awful; I could hardly stand it myself. The three chatterboxes paused, looked at each other in horror, and practically fell over each other evacuating the galley. Mission accomplished!

I chuckled to myself, *"Maybe I just found my new secret weapon!"*

37

Sixth Sense

$\mathscr{H}$ave you ever been thinking about someone whom you haven't seen in a long time and then run into them? Have you ever had a dream and it came true? Have you ever had something happen to you that you just could not explain? Coincidences? I think there has to be more to it and here are a few instances that support my theory.

I once had a dream that transpired within days. In it, I was at an airport watching the planes take off and land. I observed one particular airplane takeoff and a few minutes later I yelled, "It's coming back. Something is wrong with the airplane." I woke up with a jolt.

Later that same week, my parents and I were going on vacation to Maui. I called Aloha Airlines to reserve the tickets.

The operator said, "You're a flight attendant, right?"

I said, "Yes."

"Something is going on here at the airport; a plane had to turn around and is coming back for an emergency landing."

I was amazed because that is exactly what I dreamt. An airplane suffered structural fatigue. The fuselage of the airplane literally opened up like a tin can. Tragically, a flight attendant was sucked out of the aircraft and disappeared.

I was working an Airbus A-300 trip. Again, that is one of our largest aircraft. I was sitting on the jumpseat and for some reason visualized an aborted takeoff and my head slamming against the headrest. Ten seconds later, the pilot revved up the engines for takeoff. Halfway down the runway a warning indicator light went on in the cockpit. The captain slammed on the brakes and my head whiplashed against the jumpseat. I was stunned! I have taken off thousands and thousands of times and it is extremely rare to have an aborted takeoff.

While working a flight, a fellow flight attendant shared her encounter with her sixth sense. Liz had a bad feeling about going to work. She wanted to call in sick, but didn't feel right about it because she wasn't physically ill. She lived in Naples and had to drive to Miami on a stretch of interstate commonly referred to as Alligator Alley. Liz said she rarely speeds and always drives on the right-hand side of the road. For some reason she found herself migrating into the left lane even with no cars around to pass. A turkey vulture appeared from nowhere and slammed into her windshield on the passenger side, shattering glass everywhere. Liz was able to stay in control and pulled the car over. She sat there in shock with the dead vulture lying next to her. Had she been in the right hand lane, the bird may have hit her side of the windshield. Liz felt blessed to be alive. Needless to say, because of the incident she didn't have to work that night, after all.

My husband and I were visiting Cashiers, a small resort town nestled up in the North Carolina Mountains. My husband decided to play eighteen holes of golf giving me the opportunity to head down the mountain and visit the neighboring cities. Driving down the mountain is no picnic with winding, steep curves the whole way. Just before I reached one particular curve, I had a strong feeling to pull over. I had absolutely no reason to, but I listened to the voice. About that time I saw a semi-truck coming way too fast. His front end took up one side of the lane on the curve; his back side took up the other. I would have been forced off the road and possibly killed.

Before I got married, I was sitting in a dentist chair with a clay impression mold in my mouth. The dental hygienist was having a one way conversation with me. She was telling me she would love to fix me up with someone. They were in the Air Force together in Germany, but he was now a commercial pilot living in Fort Lauderdale, Florida. (Keep in mind, this dentist is located in Atlanta, Georgia.) "He is very handsome and a great guy," she said. "His name is Aaron Johnson." My eyes got huge. I had this stupid thing in my mouth as I was trying to tell her I was presently dating the guy she wanted to fix me up with. Coincidence? Maybe, but all of us have our own unexplained stories!

38

September 11, 2001

Everyone has a story for 9/11. Where we were, what we were doing, and how we found out. I wish I hadn't been flying that morning, but I was.

We left very early on a Super-80 aircraft out of Fort Lauderdale bound for Chicago. Due to the early outbound schedule, our airplane was one of the lucky ones to arrive at our original destination. The flight had been uneventful and we had no idea of the horror that was happening at that time.

As we were taxiing down the runway after landing, what appeared to be a Middle Eastern man rose from his seat. He continued walking toward the front of the cabin, stopping at the closet behind first class just holding his briefcase. The seatbelt sign was illuminated and even though you don't speak English, everyone knows you must remain seated. It was as if he needed to get off the airplane quickly. While strapped in his jumpseat, flight attendant number one motioned for the passenger to sit down. Obediently, he sat in the second row of coach in an empty seat.

When the aircraft finally stopped moving, the captain called the flight attendants. "Hey, you guys aren't going to believe this one. We are stuck here on the runway indefinitely and everything is shut down. That's all we know." I looked out the window and saw some kind of tower being evacuated; initially thinking something happened in Chicago.

I turned my cell phone on. It rang immediately. My husband had been trying to reach me. "What's going on?" I asked.

He said, "The authorities initially thought a commuter airplane hit the World Trade Center, but I think it was a commercial jet."

We stayed on the runway for hours. In the beginning, rumors were spreading around the aircraft. Seven airplanes had crashed in Los Angeles; Chicago's Sears Tower was supposed to be on the list. It took a while before we knew what really happened.

The first hour everyone was standing in the aisles, sharing stories of what they heard on their cell phones. None of us knew the magnitude of what occurred. We couldn't imagine who could have done such a thing. A female passenger shared she works in the World Trade Center, but happened to be in Florida.

A little later, a male passenger came to me. "A passenger sitting in 19F is making me nervous. He's the one who got up from his seat while we were taxiing. He went from seat to seat to occupy his original seat. I wanted to let you know I am concerned."

I told him I would contact the captain and let him know. This was before we knew exactly what happened. I made my way up to the cockpit and told the captain his concerns. He kind of chuckled saying, "As long as this guy isn't clutching his briefcase, I think we'll be okay." (You know in the movies, the man with a bomb has his briefcase held tightly, with copious amounts of sweat dripping down his forehead.)

As I was walking through the cabin, I looked at 19F. He did have his briefcase in his lap; everyone else had their luggage stowed under their seat or in the overhead bin. I called the captain. "Hey, guess what, he does have his briefcase in his lap." For some reason this alarmed him. This time he said seriously, "Keep an eye on him."

Two hours had passed as we maintained our professionalism and continued doing a water service. Meanwhile, another female passenger came to the galley. "I am sitting in 18D, there is a man behind me sitting in 19F who seems very suspicious to me. He doesn't ask questions, he keeps to himself, and is making me nervous." I told her I would notify the captain, then said to her in confidence, "Don't tell anyone else. We don't want to start a panic on the airplane."

At this point, the cockpit, crew and passengers all know exactly why we are grounded. Our country was under attack and we were in the middle of it. I called the captain to let him know someone else is concerned about the same passenger. This time the dismissive attitude was gone.

"If he uses the restroom, let me know," he said. "If he gets up for any reason, you let me know."

I said, "Okay."

I did another walk through the cabin. On the way, I decided to try and talk to Mr. 19F. I was slowly making my way talking to all the passengers, so it wasn't obvious that I was zeroing in on him. I arrived at his row. He was cleanly shaven wearing a blue silk shirt.

"So, are you going to be home in Chicago?" I asked. Before he could say anything, a young female passenger who was not traveling with him answered for him.

"No, he lives in Florida."

"Are you going for business or pleasure?" I continued.

Once again, she piped up and answered for him. I wasn't getting anywhere here.

During the in-flight beverage service, he asked a Spanish speaking flight attendant something in broken English. She didn't understand and asked if he spoke Spanish. He said no, so we knew he wasn't of Spanish descent.

Three hours now passed when the captain called the flight attendants, "A gate has opened for us to taxi in. I am going to call the chief of pilots to notify him of our situation."

He called a few minutes later. "The chief of pilots said we are a security risk and can't come to the gate. Someone is going to storm the aircraft from the rear of the airplane. Disarm your doors." I took a big gulp! I was the aft galley flight attendant. It would have to be my doors to disarm.

I disarmed my doors. There was a rapid knock, knock, knock! I opened the aft door with a huge adrenalin rush. Six armed men, dressed in black, burst through the door!

"Where is he, where is he?" one of them asked.

"He is sitting in 19F."

"No, go point him out to us."

Oh great! I marched down the aisle with two of the men behind me. I pointed to 19F. One of the men grabbed 19D and yanked him up.

"Not him," I said, "The other one!" (Later, 19D came to me and said it scared him so badly, he about wet himself.)

At first I felt awful. What if the passenger was completely innocent? We weren't profiling; we had no idea who could have done this horrific act of terrorism. If he wasn't exhibiting suspicious behavior, we certainly would not have known he even existed. Who gets up from his seat while the aircraft is still moving?

The security men escorted Mr. 19F off the aircraft. Everyone else, passengers and flight attendants alike, took a bus to the terminal.

The three of us flight attendants were the last to enter the airport. I slowly looked around. "Where is everyone?" It was so eerie. "What are we going to do?" I had never seen the Chicago O'Hare International Airport completely evacuated. In the distance, we saw an agent running toward us.

"Are you the crew coming from Fort Lauderdale?"

"Yes," we excitedly said.

"You need to come with me."

We were so relieved someone was looking out for us, because we would never have found a hotel on our own. Due to the grounded flights, all hotels would be full.

The agent hurried us onto a bus filled with stranded flight attendants and pilots. We took the very last and only open row. The crew sitting in front of us was Boston based. We poured out our souls to one another. We told them our story about our passenger. They told us how they were just this morning in the Boston crew operations talking and laughing with one of the ill-fated crews. They said they heard a standby flight attendant's name called out to work the Los Angeles flight. That plane was the first to hit the World Trade Center.

No hotels close to the airport had any vacancies, so it was a very long, solemn ride out of town. When we arrived, the flight attendants gathered in a room with a television watching together in horror. That was part of our family flying those airplanes. Who could have done this?

As the plot unraveled on TV, we learned most of the hijackers resided in Florida. In fact, Mohamed Atta, who flew the first plane into the tower, lived only a mile or two from my house in Delray Beach.

I flashed back to my own crisis on the airplane. If I had not made an issue of our passenger, we may have let someone of interest go free. Even if he was completely innocent, surely he could see we were just doing our job for the safety of our passengers. I am still haunted by the events of that day and often wonder about 19F.

39

On Hallowed Ground

I certainly did not want to fly after September 11. Most planes were flying nearly empty, so it appeared the public didn't either. I did notice one good thing that came from 9/11: the passengers and crewmembers were standing strong together. I had a male passenger come up to me and say, "They are going to have to get through me to get to you." I melted. Every eyeball was on each other. Everyone was on their best behavior.

A week after September 11, my first layover city was Boston, and the second night our layover city was New York. Due to the circumstances, I didn't want to go to either city. Those were, coincidentally, the trips I held in my bid the previous month.

Our hotel in New York was located in a prime location in Manhattan. We heard they were letting crewmembers go down and see Ground Zero as long as we showed our identification. The three of us decided to take the train as far as we could and walk the rest of the way. Usually, you could take the train all the way down to the World Trade Center, but on this day and for a long time after, it was closed.

I was first to notice the strange odor that filled the air. We didn't know New York City very well, but knew we were getting close to the site. We observed a large United States flag way up in the sky. That had to be the spot. The street turned a strange color of gray. I guess the soot had not been trampled on by the hustle and bustle of the city yet. We noticed layers and layers of dirt and debris on all the buildings.

When we arrived at Ground Zero, we saw the collapsed buildings. Beams pointed out at different angles; steam still rose from the ground. The police were there protecting the site from onlookers.

My eyes started to burn and sandy debris coated my teeth. Only one store remained opened — it was covered in dirt — but the Asian owner wanted to keep it open for the workers. He shared his story of how he knew most of the people in the towers because his coffee shop was across the street. "Some of my regulars are gone," he said sadly.

We walked out of the store. The stench in the air was something uniquely different. It was like an electrical smell, a rubber smell, but also the smell of death. Doom and disbelief enveloped us. I stared speechless with my hand over my mouth. How could anyone have done this? We heard the sound of a siren and saw an ambulance leave the scene. I overheard a man say another body had been found. Even now that vision is etched in my mind and in my senses. Members of my airline family perished there and to me, like so many others who lost family members, fellow firefighters, policeman and rescue personnel, it is an especially sacred place.

40

Cell Phone or Bomb?

$\mathcal{M}$y job changed after September 11. We were not only waitresses, babysitters, counselors, caretakers, doctors, nurses, and bartenders, now security guard was added to the list.

We used to have a 3-class (first class, business class and coach) domestic deluxe service on a 767 aircraft called a transcon flight from Los Angeles to Miami. I was working in business class for the arduous 5 hour trip. About half way through the service, a flight attendant working coach approached us in the mid-galley with an alarmed look on her face. She informed us that another flight attendant found a cell phone attached to a hanger in the aft lavatory. Before 9/11, we would have thought nothing of it; however, our new security training taught us that different devices could be used to detonate or be disguised as a bomb. The fact that this phone was clipped to a hanger just seemed suspicious.

We had federal marshals flying with us that day, so we asked their advice on the matter. They indeed felt it was strange that the cell phone was attached to a hanger and suggested an announcement be made to see if anyone would claim it. Flight attendant number one made the announcement in English. No one responded. Again, he made the announcement in English. Nothing. A Spanish speaking flight attendant made an announcement in Spanish. Again, no response!

The three of us business class flight attendants continued on with our duties. We were totally unaware of what activities were going on in the back of the aircraft. The coach flight attendants were busy building a bomb shelter made with blankets and other materials suggested for use in training. No one asked for our assistance, so we had no idea what they were doing. Next thing I knew the captain called and said we were diverting to Dallas.

I said in a humorous tone, "Wait a minute, I need to make my commuter flight to Atlanta." I just felt there could be a solution to the unclaimed cell phone. The flight attendants gathered around the coach galley to discuss the situation. "Why don't I go down one aisle and someone else go down the other and ask each person point blank if they have their cell phone?" I suggested. The number one flight attendant volunteered. Down the aisles we went. "Do you have your cell phone? Do you have your cell phone? Do you have your cell phone?"

Flight attendant number one approached a sleeping Japanese man. "Excuse me sir, are you missing a cell phone?" He didn't speak any English, but his bi-lingual Japanese partner translated for us. The now awake but groggy man searched his pockets and a sheepish grin appeared on his face. "Yeees!" We found him!

We brought the fellow to the aft galley area to identify his device and show him the chaos he had unknowingly created. We retrieved his phone and thankfully continued with our flight pattern toward Miami. I made my commuter flight to Atlanta and reflected once again on that horrible day and how it had changed our world.

41

Haunted Hotel

$\mathscr{R}$ecently, I stayed at a beautiful ornate hotel in San Antonio, where I was awakened by my alarm clock at 3:15 a.m. My routine for getting up for an early sign-in is rather standard. I turn on CNN Headline News, make my coffee, and then take a shower.

After a hot shower, I poured a cup of coffee and just then the TV suddenly went mute. I turned the volume up and continued putting on my makeup while watching the news. To my amazement, the channels were changing by themselves. The remote control was on the other side of the bed.

I looked around the room feeling uneasy. I gazed upward and saw old, old pipes. *This hotel is haunted.* It must have been a male ghost, because like most males he wanted control of the remote!

I dressed quickly and headed to the lobby. Two gentlemen were working the front desk.

"Hey you guys, how old is this hotel?"

One clerk said, "It is over a hundred years old."

I asked, "Is it haunted."

They looked at each other and snickered. "Oh yeah," they both chimed.

One of the gentlemen recalled an early morning only two weeks ago where a maid had called him at the front desk. She tried to open the door to the laundry room in the basement, but it was locked. It never had been locked previously. He searched the drawers for any keys that could possibly open the door and to his surprise found one that said laundry room. He went downstairs, tried the key and it did not work. After trying the key again, he was disappointed it didn't open the door. Just as he and the maid were about to give up, they heard something from inside the room. The floor was your typical cement basement floor. Coming toward them was a distinct sound of a lady walking in high heel shoes. The footsteps turned and headed to the center of the room. They tried the key one more time. It opened right up, but no one was in the room.

The other hotel attendant led me to the kitchen. He showed me where he was standing when his encounter occurred.

"Do you see the end of the kitchen?" he asked. "You and I went through the only entrance to the room. I saw a man standing at the opposite far end of the kitchen. I thought he was a homeless man who had somehow entered the building and wandered into the kitchen. As I slowly approached to confront him, he just disappeared! No one was there. I saw him," he said adamantly.

"People are seen in the ballroom dancing as it was back in the 1930s," he continued. "They are dressed as if attending a costume party. One was spotted holding a mask in front of his face." He said on the 10th floor a man was spotted several times in his tuxedo. Pretty cool and *Very spooky!*

42

Diabetic or Drunk?

"*G*ood morning," I said in a happy voice to all the passengers coming aboard. It was an early morning flight, and I am my best in the morning. I realize not everyone is like me, so I am not offended when I hear a grunt from someone or even a look of disgust. Every once in a while, I board someone who is like me and we immediately click.

Johnny, a passenger in his mid-30s, was one such passenger. He was a handsome guy wearing jeans and a sweatshirt. Johnny stepped on the aircraft eating trail mix. I commented on how healthy that looked. He flashed a heartwarming smile. As he stopped to talk to me, he showed signs of light-headedness and grabbed the closet door. I took his elbow and guided him to an empty first class seat.

"Are you on any medication?" I asked.

"No, I am diabetic," he muttered. Johnny showed signs of agitation, but tried to smile.

"Can I bring you some orange juice?" I asked.

Still somewhat coherent, he shook his head no. The other flight attendant said there was no way Johnny was in any shape to travel. We told the captain we had a problem.

I checked on Johnny who said he'd better take the orange juice now. He took a sip, but was shaking so hard it spilled all over him and the seat. His head was jerking back and forth as he frantically rubbed his thighs. I thought maybe he had multiple sclerosis. I asked him again if he had been drinking or was taking any stimulants. Johnny said no.

A female passenger sitting in first class said she didn't want him to come with us, "He's drunk!"

I stopped to check on Johnny. He was pounding his fists up and down, laughing uncontrollably. I had never seen anything like it. I reported to the captain. I told him maybe I should give the passenger some oxygen because it seemed as though he was becoming incoherent. "Paramedics are on the way," he said.

I returned to Johnny once again.

"What are you feeling?" I asked. While he was jerking his head around, he managed to spout out a few words.

"I feel itchy all over," he said. "I can't stop laughing."

Both of us felt helpless. I told him paramedics were on the way. He shook his head with relief.

I looked again and Johnny was popping trail mix in his mouth like a madman. Only half made it into his mouth.

Finally, the paramedics showed up with a ton of equipment. They asked us for something sweet. The flight attendant working first class gave them a cookie off one of the first class trays. We stopped the boarding process so the paramedics could do their job.

In a matter of minutes they started packing their equipment.

"Hey, what's going on?" I asked.

"Oh, he'll be fine," the one paramedic said nonchalantly, "He waited too late to take his insulin."

I was shocked! That's it? I was amazed along with everyone else. It was a major learning experience for me.

We let Johnny stay in first class and he was totally normal throughout the whole flight. I joked with him, "What some passengers will do to get a free first class upgrade!" We both laughed but it certainly was a memorable start to the day.

43

Mexico City

$\mathscr{M}$exico City is known for being one of the largest cities in the world with inexpensive shopping, great Mexican cuisine and extremely high pollution. On one occasion, while riding in the van to the hotel, our van driver said it is not uncommon to see a bird drop from the sky because the air is so bad. Unfortunately, the city is also reputed to have a high crime rate.

I was flying with a captain who had just flown to Mexico City. He and the first officer decided to have dinner downtown. The cab driver seemed to be a trustworthy guy, so the pilots asked if he would stay until they finished their meal, then return them to the hotel. They would make sure he was well compensated. Of course, the cab driver agreed.

After finishing their meal, they stepped into the cab. The captain was familiar with the city and soon realized they were heading in the wrong direction of the hotel. He asked the driver where he was going. "No speaka English, no speaka English," he replied. The driver didn't have any problems speaking English earlier.

The car was definitely heading out of the city. Thinking quickly, the captain took off his belt, put it around the driver's neck and gave it a tug. "Take us back to the hotel, *NOW*!" he demanded.

Panicked, the driver hesitantly made a U-turn. The car behind him flashed his lights. It was obvious that it was part of a setup. The cab driver returned the pilots to the hotel safe and sound. Thank God the captain thought quickly. Who knows what could have happened to them!

44

SARS

*F*light attendants are exposed to every kind of illness. We are in direct contact with thousands of people. They hand us cups, cans, napkins, newspapers and even used tissues. People are coughing and sneezing and it's pretty much impossible to fully protect ourselves from contagious diseases.

When the SARS epidemic broke out, we learned that we could actually die from inhaling the germs of an infected person. We could die from other diseases through intimate contact, but this was something unique. Free flowing, contaminated air particles could kill us.

Coincidentally during the epidemic scare, other typical flu-like symptoms were rampant. One of the cities hit hard with SARS was Toronto. Ironically, that is where I was flying for the month!

Before my 3-day trip, my throat felt tender. I debated going to work at all, but thought it might go away. That was a huge mistake because it was an exhausting, multi-leg trip. My sore throat turned into a cold. For the next two days I was sniffling and sneezing. After the trip was over, I was waiting for the employee van in the cold, windy night air. For some reason the van was twenty minutes late and I completely lost my voice.

The next day, I was coughing up yellow mucous. I kept thinking it would get better, but it only got worse. My chest began to hurt so badly, I went to see the doctor.

"Does your chest hurt?" The doctor asked.

"Yes."

"Are you coughing?"

"Yes."

"Do you have a fever?"

"I don't think so," I replied.

He took X-rays and returned with a sorrowful look. "You have a small mass on your lung," he reported. "It looks like you have pneumonia." I stared at him with eyes wide open and gasped. This was not a word you wanted to hear especially with the SARS epidemic going around. He prescribed antibiotics for seven days.

After taking the antibiotics faithfully, I was still not well. I stopped by the clinic to see if there was anything else I could do. The doctor said he had been thinking of me for the entire week. This was the first time in his career where he could possibly have been exposed to a life-threatening illness by being in the same room as his patient. The fact that I was a flight attendant flying to Toronto didn't help the situation. He hesitantly gave me antibiotics for three more days.

Finally, the coughing stopped and I slowly got better. I was pretty scared. Both the doctor and I were very much relieved.

45

Held Hostage

A full blue moon. *Very unusual*, I thought, as I looked up at the sky from the top deck of our house. It was 3 a.m., as I sipped my coffee. *I hope that doesn't bring out the beast in people*, I mused. My Himalayan cats looked up at me with great sadness in their eyes — please don't leave us again. They saw the suitcase packed and my uniform on, so they knew I would be gone for another couple of days.

I drove the usual fifty minutes to the airport and boarded the 6 a.m. commuter flight from Atlanta to Miami. After arriving, I took my time getting off the airplane as I still had plenty to spare until my working flight began.

I knew the captain who was flying the airplane, so I stopped in the cockpit to chat. He had an alarmed look on his face.

"All of our airplanes are grounded," he said.

My heart sank, "Not another terrorist attack!"

"No, no, not that," he said assuredly. "Some kind of computer glitch."

Our airline could not retrieve any information such as passenger loads or gate information, not to mention flight plans. I could not even sign-in for my trip.

It took about three hours to fix the problem, but three hours is a long time to ground airplanes. This, along with weather, snowballed into one of the most hellish days in airline history.

The first day of our trip we were to fly three legs: Miami-Atlanta, Atlanta-Miami, Miami-Atlanta. With all the computer problems that morning, we managed to leave at 11:30 a.m. with only an hour delay. By the time we arrived in Atlanta, the system was running further behind.

We would now be leaving Atlanta two hours late. The gate agents started boarding passengers on our Super-80 aircraft around 3:45 p.m. We took off thirty minutes later heading for Miami for a one hour and twenty five minute flight. After about fifty minutes into the flight, I felt the plane doing a little maneuvering. My body feels heavy when this happens; it also makes me feel a little light-headed.

After completing our beverage service, the flight attendants gathered in the first class galley for a chat session. The captain called and said he needed to use the restroom. As he came out, he stated that Miami is getting hit with a torrential thunderstorm. The airport is now closed, so we'll be circling in the interim.

It seemed like forever as we circled in our holding position. The captain made an announcement that due to our fuel situation, we would have to divert to our alternate city, which is Tampa. A few minutes later the PA was heard, "Flight attendants, prepare for landing."

Several passengers were hungry and asked if they could get off the airplane in Tampa. I told them I would do my best to convince the agents; after all, the last time I had eaten anything was around noon. It was now close to 7 p.m. This flight was a beverage service only in both cabins. We had nothing to offer but pretzels.

The captain taxied the airplane to the gate. The agents said everyone must remain onboard. I looked out the window to see the 767s, 757s and 737s, all getting refueled. We were all stuck in Tampa together waiting patiently for Miami's weather to clear.

The other flight attendant, Annie, and I tried to make the best of an ugly situation. We filled trays with OJ and water and hand delivered them to our full load of passengers. Fifty minutes had gone by and then another forty minutes. The agent managed to get us four more bags of pretzels. I apologized to each person as I handed out their "dinner." I thought the passengers were taking the situation pretty well. A lot of them called their loved ones in Miami verifying the fact it was like a hurricane there.

The sun went down as we begrudgingly sat at the gate. We had been on the plane for a total of five hours so far. Finally, we heard the engines sputter. The seatbelt sign came on. "Hurry," I said, "Take your seats; it's time to go." With utter anticipation, everyone who had been standing scrambled to their seats.

The captain said it would take a while for us to depart because there were a lot of airplanes in front of us. At this point we didn't care, as long as we were moving. Once again the captain's voice was heard, "We are number three for takeoff. Flight attendants, prepare for takeoff." Everyone cheered!

We took off for our thirty minute flight to Miami. The turbulence was quite fierce, but we arrived safely. It was now 10 p.m. I couldn't wait to get something to eat. Visions of all my choices were popping up in my head: pizza, chicken with rice, anything hot and comforting would do. I usually bring all kinds of food with me, but on that day I brought nothing.

We sat on the runway for some time. The dreaded captain's voice returned. "Well, we apologize ladies and gentlemen; they are telling us it's going to be another fifty minutes." Everyone sighed — including me.

Passengers were up from their seats. Annie and I had given away pretty much everything we had. The ice drawer was now water with a few remnants of ice chips. Fifty minutes came and went. The captain explained there were twenty one aircrafts full of people waiting just like us. Everything was at a standstill. Planes were parked at the gates with no flight crews because the flight crews were on the planes waiting to come in. They didn't have the manned ground crew to transfer bags. Everything that could go wrong, went wrong.

Meanwhile, the once patient and understanding passengers were now facing a reality: we are trapped on this airplane and we can't get off. Annie and I were sympathetic. I assured the passengers in the years I have been flying, nothing like this had ever happened.

I sat on my jumpseat to rest for a minute. I saw a man approaching me with all the signs of an outraged, fed up passenger. "What would happen if I opened up that exit? No kidding, I have had it," he huffed. I was very much identifying with his anger. I smiled at him and showered him with kindness assuring him that we can't stay here forever. This seemed to appease him for the moment as he returned to his seat.

Once again, an announcement was made of no progress. Passengers now lost all sense of dignity. I heard a passenger call 911. "What do you mean this is not an emergency? How many hours is it going to take before this is an emergency?" Click! From what I understood, calls to news channels, The Miami Herald, the police station, and attempts to reach our airlines' president were made. I looked at my watch, quarter to twelve. I pulled a muscle in my leg earlier, I hadn't eaten for twelve hours, and I was exhausted.

"Why can't we park at another airlines' gate?"

"Why can't they send a bus to pick us up?"

"Am I going to make my South America connection?"

"What happens to my bags if my flight cancels tonight and I have to fly tomorrow?"

All of the questions were legitimate questions; I had no answers. I relayed everything that was asked to the captain. He too was getting fed up.

The passengers began to chant. "WE WANT OFF, WE WANT OFF!" Call lights were purposely being pushed with frustration. I called the captain to let him in on the action. "You might want to hear this," I said.

A few passengers were eyeballing the exits. One asked which exit would be the best to blow. I told him none of them would be good to blow. You definitely would not want to open the aft tail cone exit. You have to walk out on a catwalk, and then find the inflation handle to blow the slide. When you do find the handle, you must look for the silver pillow packs to ensure that the slide did indeed blow. His enthusiasm began to fade. "Well, how long are we supposed to be out here before we take matters into our own hands?" I didn't have any answers. I felt their pain!

The captain had the chief of pilots on the phone. It was getting pretty ugly. We had two families with babies. The mother came to me in the galley. "I have no more diapers. What am I supposed to do?" I am not a mother but deeply sympathized with her. I told her we have stay-free maxi pads. Truly, I thought that was better than a poopy diaper. She probably knew at that point I wasn't a mom and turned and walked away.

Finally, we heard the engines revving up, and the seatbelt sign came on. "Hurry," I said. "Take your seats; it's time to go." This time they looked at me with skeptical looks on their faces, but obediently took their seats. We finally parked at our gate at 12:18 a.m.

We had a young boy who was not accompanied by an adult flying with us. The parents pay our airline a small fee and we basically watch over them during the flight. Normally, there are special agents who meet the flight and take the unaccompanied child to their loved ones. Unfortunately, there wasn't anyone this night. The frustrated gate agent said I would have to take him. The little boy called his mother to let her know we had arrived. We assumed she would be right outside security, but she wasn't there. I told Annie I would check on the hotel situation if she would escort the boy to find his mother.

Normally at 12:30 a.m., the airport is empty. Looking around it seemed like mid-day. Stranded families stopped me with their hands reaching out, pleading for me to help them. I couldn't. Not that I didn't want to, but I simply didn't have any answers. I was hungry and tired myself, but my heart went out to them.

I made my way to our operations area. Stranded flight attendants with no hotels were everywhere. I was on hold for thirty minutes waiting for someone to pick-up my call to our hotel/limo desk. Finally, I got a human voice. All the flight attendants swarmed me. "Let me talk, let me talk," they yelled. The man on the phone found a hotel thirty-five minutes away. We didn't care where it was; we just wanted to sleep. The hour of 2 a.m. now passed. I looked up and saw Annie still attached to the unaccompanied minor. She couldn't find his mom anywhere. Her cell phone went to voice mail; perhaps she had a dead battery. We handed the boy off to the manager on duty and headed for ground transportation.

All the stranded flight attendants hurriedly piled in the bus. Probably around thirty of us total. No one said a word for quite a while. Then the silence was broken by someone yelling, "Does anyone have an empty bag?" I looked up and saw Annie, pale as a ghost. She was so fatigued and exhausted that it made her physically sick. We all sat there in a daze while poor Annie threw up.

Finally, we arrived at the hotel at 3 a.m. The hotel clerk was overwhelmed at seeing all of us. It took him forever. So, at 3:30 a.m., I saw the most wonderful bed I had ever seen in my life (tacky, blue-checked bedspread and all).

As I lay in bed, I kept replaying the day's events. Did I do everything I could to make things better? I hope I didn't say anything wrong?

A little over 24 hours ago, I was on my balcony, sipping my coffee gazing up at that full blue moon. I remember thinking, *I hope that doesn't bring out the craziness in people*. Hmm, maybe there is something to a full moon after all.

46

Near-Death Experiences

*N*ear-death experiences fascinate me and are one of my favorite topics of conversation. I am so intrigued by people who say they have actually died and come back to tell about it. I have talked to several people who have given me their firsthand account.

A fellow flight attendant shared his story. He was having an operation performed on the first floor of the hospital. He somehow disengaged from his body and floated to the third floor but was able to witness the operation. While on that floor, he could hear the conversations of the nurses taking place. When he regained consciousness after the operation, he saw one of the nurses. "So, how is your son doing?" he asked. "And did you get all of your laundry done last night?" The nurse was absolutely flabbergasted as there was no way he could have known about her son or their conversation.

Another passenger told me her near-death experience. She was having a baby. During the delivery, a complication occurred and the doctor lost her for a while. When she died, she saw a closed door with brilliant beams of light coming from the inside. She was afraid to open the door. As she got closer and almost opened it, she came back to her body.

I was telling a flight attendant how much I feared drowning or being burned alive. She said she actually drowned before and it wasn't that bad. She had been drinking with her boyfriend and his friend on a dock at the lake. Their happy hour turned unhappy. Her boyfriend picked her up and said in a fun way, "I'm going to throw you in." He indeed did. She knew how to swim, but she was tipsy. As she sank to the bottom, she couldn't figure out which direction was up. She took one gulp of water and that was it. I always pictured drowning victims as frantically gasping for air, but she said she didn't. All she felt was an incredible feeling of peace. Her boyfriend and friend were able to bring her back to life.

A young mother named Judy told me her daughter's story. Her two children were having fun playing in the pool, while she, her husband, and brother were getting some sun. Her son was 3 years old and her daughter was 5 years old. The little boy said, "Look at me, look at me." As they were giving their son complete attention, they realized their daughter was nowhere to be found. Judy knew something was wrong. She jumped up and looked at the bottom of the pool. Nothing. She ran in the house, but still couldn't find her. Again, she returned to the pool and noticed a floating raft.

After lifting it up, she found her daughter lying face down not breathing. She yelled at her husband and brother to call 911. They froze for a second. After snapping out of shock, the brother ran next door to their neighbor's house. Her neighbor was a physician and was able to get her daughter breathing again, but she was unconscious all the way to the hospital. When her daughter woke up, she looked at Judy and the first thing she said was, "I touched God's sandals, Mommy."

Rachel, another fellow flight attendant, told me her story. Her mother had passed away a few years prior. Two days after she died, her father said the lamp that was only used by her mom came on. Rachel told him maybe mom was trying to make contact from the other side.

Two days after that, just before the funeral Rachel woke up to find her own bedroom light on. She knew she didn't leave it on when she went to sleep. She asked her mom if that was her. The light went off. Rachel said she heard her mother's voice say, "Clear your head, Rachel." She said she wasn't afraid at all. The light came back on. Her mother said, "I loved your father, I loved my five children, and I loved my five grandchildren." Then the light went off again. A second or two passed and the light came back on. "I am in the light and I am at peace. I will help you with your father." Again, the light shut off. One last time the light came back on only to hear her mother's last words: "Believe, trust and pray." Then the light turned off.

I was talking to a young, African-American passenger who was in the military. I asked if his parents were still here. He shook his head no. His mother had passed a few years prior. I asked if he was there when she passed. He was in the hospital with her, and when she died he felt her pat him on the back as she departed.

From what I have heard, death is an easy, spiritual transition. You are in your body one moment and in another dimension the next. Heaven has been described with blazing colors that diminish the most vibrant of our earthly shades. Unimaginable beauty surrounds one and you are filled with an immense feeling of peace and contentment. Recognizable loved ones or guardian angels are there with you to guide you in the transition. We will all find out soon enough but from what I can tell, I don't think death is anything to fear.

47

Late for his Own Funeral

*O*ne of the most dangerous things that can happen to an aircraft on takeoff and landing is to hit a bird. You wouldn't think these feathered creatures could do so much damage, but they can. The miracle on the Hudson River is a prime example of what can happen.

I flew with a captain who told me his frightening experience. He was taking off when several birds flew right into the engine. Shrapnel went everywhere, shredding the engine. The steering wheel was shaking so violently it took all of his strength to hold it steady to circle back to the runway. The flight attendants could see outdoors through the bottom of the galley door. They said the plane sounded like a giant silverware drawer being shaken up and down. No one was injured.

Our bird incident wasn't so dramatic, but it was eventful. Upon arrival in Tampa, we hit a huge crane. It left about a quarter-inch dent on the wing. The captain called the maintenance department, and the assessment was not good. According to the FAA, the dent exceeded the minimum amount a fuselage can be damaged. The aircraft would have to go out of service.

This was the last flight departing from Tampa. The passengers had already boarded and we were ready to depart to New York. An elderly woman sitting in first class seemed overly distraught. I went to her to see if I could be of any assistance. She explained her husband passed away and his body was in the cargo department. I got a chill knowing there was a corpse right below us. She went on to say his funeral was scheduled early tomorrow morning in New York.

I hated to have to tell this already grieving woman the flight was cancelled. There were no other flights with us or any other carrier. Tragically for this family that poor man was going to fulfill the cliché and in fact be late for his own funeral.

48

That's Not Dust, That's Smoke

May 17, 2006. It was a 2-day trip, with a layover in Austin. The best part about this trip was that I would be flying with my good friend, Terry. Usually I have a feeling if something bad is going to happen on my flight, but I think because I looked forward to seeing my friend, I wasn't aware of any negative vibes. I met the captain at the gate in Atlanta going to Dallas/ Fort Worth. His name was Tim.

I asked, "When is the plane going to arrive?"

He looked at me and said with a smile, "How should I know?"

I pointed to the four stripes on his shirt and counted, "One-Two-Three-Four."

He pointed to his four stripes and counted, "I-Don't-Know-Anything." We both cracked up laughing.

He said, "I can tell I am going to get along with you just fine." Little did we know this trip would bond us for the rest of our lives and Captain Tim would be my hero!

Our first leg was ATL-D/FW, the second D/FW-Nashville, the third Nashville-D/FW, and our last leg was D/FW-Austin. We made it to Dallas okay, but our Nashville leg was unfortunately, very eventful. We never made it to Austin.

While in D/FW, we boarded our three quarters full airplane on a Super-80 aircraft bound for Nashville, and pushed back from the gate. Lorraine, our number one flight attendant, began to make her PA announcements, letting Terry and I know it was time to do our manual safety demonstration with the seatbelt, safety card, and mask. Before we began the demo, Terry said a passenger stopped her and asked if she smelled anything burning. All three of us immediately stopped what we were doing and went about the cabin with our noses in the air.

I walked from the front of the aircraft, where I immediately smelled an electrical odor, to the very back row where I didn't smell anything at all. As I walked to the forward part of the cabin, I could smell it faintly at row 12, but stronger in first class. All three of us detectives decided the most pungent area was first class. No passengers were sitting in the aisle seats of 4B or 5B, so Terry climbed on 5B and said she believed it was strongest above 5AB's overhead bin. I climbed up on 4B and took a whiff of 4AB and then 5AB. No doubt about it: It was definitely above 5AB. We informed Captain Tim. He didn't hesitate to return to the gate.

As soon as we opened the aircraft door, the mechanics immediately drew their bodies back. "Wooo, do you smell that?" The agent made a PA announcement requesting all passengers deplane with carryon items and bags. Due to the situation, I was sure the agent thought as we did, this plane would go out of service.

We all congregated in the first class area: the mechanics, cockpit and the flight attendants. We told the maintenance team exactly where we thought the smell originated. The mechanics opened several compartments and panels but couldn't find anything. I climbed on the seat several times saying, "Here, smell this; its right here." I climbed down. The pilots apparently enjoyed it because I hadn't realized that every time my arms stretched towards the overhead bin, my dress also reached up. We joked around some more while the mechanics tried to figure out the origin of the odor.

Once again, I stepped on the side of the cushion and this time shouted, "I found it. There is a crackling noise above the overhead bin!"

Finally, the mystery was solved; it had to do something with the lights. The maintenance team took out the fluorescent light tube where the coupler attached was sizzling; smoke freely flowing in a spiral effect.

"Okay," the mechanic said.

"Okay what?" I asked. "This plane is going out of service, right?"

"No, you can go," he said.

I couldn't believe my ears. "I just saw smoke with my own eyes and you think it's safe to take off? What if it affected the wiring or other parts of the aircraft?"

Our mechanics do a wonderful job and normally I wouldn't question their judgment, but I asked Tim if he felt okay flying this airplane. "We'll get the air turned on, check into it and see what happens." After turning on the air circulation, the odor did seem to diminish. So we boarded the passengers on the same aircraft.

A dark-skinned female with beautiful curls dangling about her face boarded the airplane. "Don't worry," she told me. "I said some major prayers in the terminal and we'll be fine." That was actually quite comforting.

We had an 8-year-old unaccompanied minor named Heather traveling with us. The first time we boarded, her seat was in coach. She was visiting her dad for a couple of weeks.

I approached her with a smile, "Have you traveled before?"

"Yes," she nodded.

"My name is Chris, if you need anything, let me know."

She seemed distant and non-emotional. We had an empty seat in first class, so I asked if she would like to sit there.

Heather didn't say a word but gathered all of her things and acted like it was no big deal. I sat her down in 3F. I said, "You know people pay a lot of money to sit up here." She gave me a half smile, but still not a word.

After everyone boarded the airplane, we pushed away from the gate with another attempt to Nashville. As we were doing our safety demonstration, I thought I may have smelled the same odor again. I asked a few passengers in first class if they smelled anything, but they said no.

So, we took off. I was sitting on my jumpseat in the back of the aircraft. The phone chimed twice. It was the captain. "Do you guys smell anything?" At that moment, a beam of sunlight from the exit door window seemed rather thick right in front of me — like a thick cloud of dust. On closer inspection, I realized it looked like fog churning about. Then it dawned on me: *That's not dust, that's smoke!* Where my jumpseat was located, I turned around and peered into the cabin. Smoke was everywhere. I relayed the information to the captain. "We're turning around," he said briskly.

The airplane took a turn to the left. For some reason, Terry's phone in the very back of the cabin didn't work. She was trying to hand signal that she saw the smoke. Terry and I quickly went into our emergency training mode. "Terry, you grab the fire extinguishers, and I'll try to find the source of the smoke."

I quickly walked to the forward part of the cabin checking the overhead bins along the way for warmth from a fire. They felt cold, so I opened up every bin to see if there might be visible smoke. I motioned Lorraine to turn off anything electrical; she said, "I already did." We checked the lavatories for smoke but didn't see anything.

It must have been pretty frightening for passengers to see the flight attendants walking around with fire extinguishers. Several women were screaming and crying. One of them was the person who said a prayer for us. Another was putting her fists to her head while tears streamed down her face. "We're going to die, we're going to die," she cried out.

I looked out one of the windows and realized we were getting close to the ground, so I headed for my jumpseat. I assured the hysterical women the extinguishers were only for precaution.

We followed our training procedures to the letter. Unfortunately, one of our procedures states when there is smoke in the cabin you must evacuate. I pulled Terry aside and said, "Listen, the smoke has subsided; I don't think we need to evacuate."

She looked at me, shocked, with an expression like "evacu-what." She said, "I haven't even thought about that yet." She agreed though that the smoke had diminished greatly.

Lorraine, being the number one flight attendant, had the most contact with the pilots in an emergency. I told her the same thing as Terry, "Tell the captain when he asks, the smoke seems to have subsided." She looked at me with the same expression as Terry only her mouth dropped open. This was the closest I had ever been to an evacuation. The thought wasn't too appealing to me either.

I sat on my jumpseat with everyone staring and studying me. I tried to act calm and confident. I looked at my exit door. If I was to hear the right signal from the cockpit, I would jump up from my seat, look through the tiny exit door window and determine if there were any non-favorable conditions, such as smoke or fire. If all clear, I would turn the exit door handle and swing the door open. I've heard it is sometimes difficult to open the door, so I would have to rock it to pop the slide. Sometimes the slide doesn't open at all. In that case, I have to pull a handle on the bottom of the door to disengage the slide. If the slide opens, I need to tell two people to be my assistants. They will stay at the bottom of the slide and help the people off. If the slide doesn't open, it is a blocked exit. I would grab a person and tell him or her to stay there and guard the exit. Don't let anyone jump. I then stand on a seat and redirect passengers to useable exits. If it is a useable slide to which I've assigned two assistants, then I have to start the evacuation by saying commands. This particular door is a single aisle door, so my commands are fairly easy. "Jump. Don't take anything with you."

The passenger next to my jumpseat wanted to have a chat session. As he was talking, his words became blah, blah, blah, blah, blah, blah, blah. Seeing that he was able-bodied, little did he know, I was sizing him up as my potential assistant. I glanced at the exit one more time.

The plane seemed to be going too fast for landing. I put my hand on the aisle seat armrest to brace myself. With much relief, we landed. With even more relief, I heard no signal to evacuate. It took Captain Tim only six minutes to turn the airplane around and land! The pilots did an incredible job! In fact, we landed so quickly, the fire department didn't have time to follow us in for landing, so we waited on the runway for the fire trucks to approach us to let us know our aircraft looked good from the outside.

At the gate, the passengers again gathered their belongings and deplaned. I saw the mechanic, who mistakenly said, "It's okay to go." I pointed my finger at him and sharply said, "I told you this plane should not have taken off." I was still shaken. I took a deep breath and calmed myself down. "You have no idea what a nightmare we've been through," I told the mechanic. "This is what happened…"

I walked into the terminal with our passengers, staring quietly. My attention was broken when I heard someone calling my name. "Chris! Chris!" The little unaccompanied minor grabbed my waist. She clung to my side as I put my arm around her and touched my head to hers. We stood there silently. Heather didn't seem afraid; in fact, she looked at the emergency situation as an adventure. So much for thinking she had no emotions.

A flight service supervisor was there to meet the flight attendants. She made sure we were okay and handed us the paperwork. We hate any kind of eventful situations because there is always the paperwork to fill out at the end.

After finding a new aircraft and hiking to the gate on the other side of the terminal, we boarded our flight once again to good ole Nashville, Tennessee. As the passengers came on, I tried to make light of the situation, "You again," or "Okay, this is the last time I am going to take your jacket." They seemed to appreciate the humor. One of the hysterical women looked a lot calmer. I put my arms out to give her a big hug. She hugged me with all of her might. I noticed later she was sprawled out in her seat sleeping with her mouth wide opened. The guy next to her said she took some Xanax. *No wonder!*

After doing the safety demonstration and seatbelt checks, I sat down on my jumpseat exhausted and could feel the adrenalin drain from me. I was ready to call it a day. The last thing I wanted to do was go to Nashville and then fly back to D/FW. Because of the delay, we knew our Austin leg was cancelled, which meant our day would be done in D/FW.

For the third time, we taxied down the runway. After we took off, the captain called again. *Now what,* I thought! "Uhhh, there is some kind of smell in the cockpit and I need you to climb on my seat to see where it is coming from." He was referring to my dress hiking up. After all that happened, we were still able to joke around with each other. "In all seriousness," he said, "You guys did an awesome job. Had we taken off the first time with that smoking light who knows what would have happened? It could have been really serious."

Later on, Tim made a PA announcement commending the flight attendants' performance. Everyone applauded. I looked down in embarrassment. As we did the beverage service, several people thanked us for everything. While picking up cups, people clapped as I walked by. It brought tears to my eyes. It still does. A little recognition goes a long way.

After we landed, a male passenger grabbed hold of my arm. "I have to tell you there are some flight attendants you enjoy watching work," he said. "You are one of them." I smiled and thought; these moments are the flying highs.

49

The Voice

*E*ven though I loved living in Atlanta, the commute was taking a toll on me. My husband and I missed the palm trees and beaches, so we moved from Georgia back to Florida.

It was an early morning flight from West Palm Beach to D/FW. The plane was packed as usual with only a spattering of empty seats. Just before departure, a young man dressed in a white muscle shirt came barreling down the aisle completely out of breath. His shaved head was covered with sweat dripping down onto his bulging tattooed muscles. He was carrying a number of oversized duffle bags. All the passengers' eyes followed him to the back of the aircraft with an obviously disapproving and disgusted look. My initial thought was, *I wonder why on earth the agents let him on the airplane with all those oversized bags.*

He made his way back to the very last row and placed some of his bags on the seat. He opened the overhead bin above his seat and saw that it was full. He opened another one that was also full. I jumped in and started opening up the bins until I found one I could rearrange to accommodate his luggage. He crammed his bags in the overhead bin and drenched in sweat, headed to his seat.

I retreated to the galley, thinking how inconsiderate he was. I went above and beyond to help him and he didn't even thank me. I went on and on in my own negative thoughts. I glanced at him while he struggled to catch his breath as sweat poured down his body.

All of a sudden a voice came deep from inside me that said, "Don't judge him; be kind to him." I stopped dead in my tracks. I wanted to ask the other passengers, "Did you just hear that?" You know how I am with my inner voice and immediately obeyed. I poured him a glass of water and handed him paper towels for his sweat. He slept for the entire flight.

Two days later, I was now working D/FW back to West Palm Beach. Renee, the flight attendant I was working with, asked if I remembered the muscle man we had on our flight two days prior.

I nodded my head yes.

"Well, he's on our flight again today. He said his friend had committed suicide and he was the one that found him dead. He was heading to Dallas for the funeral. Those huge bags he was carrying were his departed friend's belongings to give to his family."

I thought back to how I initially judged him like everyone else, but was so thankful I didn't act on my emotions.

I went up to him and said long time no see. He looked at me with humble gratitude. "Hey, you're the flight attendant who was so nice to me." I told him because of his circumstances, I am glad I was.

This was such an important lesson to me: you never know what someone is going through personally and how important it is to be kind to people no matter what.

50

Rebecca

$\mathcal{I}$ was in Miami International Airport by the gate taking tickets from the passengers for our flight to San Francisco. A flight service manager approached me: "Hey, have you heard about Rebecca? She was flying the same trip you are on, two days earlier, and passed away in her room in San Francisco." I asked for Rebecca's last name, but she didn't remember.

I continued pulling tickets. Rebecca, Rebecca, the only Rebecca I knew was my good friend Rebecca, but she was way too young. I pictured a flight attendant in her 50s, 60s, maybe even 70s. Not someone in her 40s.

My friend Terri, whom I was flying with, left the aircraft to pull up the flight schedule of two days ago to see if we could solve the mystery. I joined her at the computer as all passengers were now on board. I was sure I wouldn't know her. I gazed at the number one position. My knees buckled, tears filled my eyes. I gasped! There was her name. It was my Rebecca.

Rebecca and I flew together three months earlier. Her big, beautiful blue eyes and strawberry-blonde hair was her trademark, and she had a young son who was her life. I loved flying with her. She had swapped one of her trips we were on that month. "If I had known you were going to be flying with me," she said. "I would never have traded it." She was divorced from her husband, but remained amicable with him and had a new boyfriend who was very good to her.

On the way to San Francisco, I thought of her the whole trip. I wanted to know what happened to my friend. "How, when, why?"

We arrived at the Sheraton hotel. I asked the front desk clerk what happened to Rebecca.

"She didn't show up for the van pick up, so one of the flight attendants and security guard went to check on her," he said. "That's when they discovered she had passed away."

She was 46 years old.

"Which room was she was in?" I asked.

"Well, her room has not been released yet because it has only been two days, but she was in room 909," the clerk replied.

I looked down at my key. *Hmm, 910.* I was saying earlier on the plane I wouldn't mind if Rebecca came to visit me in my room, I would like to say goodbye to her. The other flight attendants said, "Not me." They didn't know her, and they didn't want to be visited by her from the other side.

The flight attendants walked down the hall together. "915, 914, 913, 912, 911, 910." I stopped at 910. Right next to me was room 909. Terri looked at me with her eyebrow lifted as I walked into my room. Almost to say, "You asked for it." I heard a moaning wind tunnel under my doorway as I closed it. *Uhh, that's a little spooky.*

I opened my suitcase, pulled out my pajamas, and quickly put them on. I looked at the door adjoining my room. "Wow, that was Rebecca's room." She was the last person to lie in that bed. I pictured her in that heavenly signature bed Sheraton hotels are known for.

I normally have no trouble sleeping, but this night was different. I kept having flashbacks of the two of us flying together. I recalled putting my arms around her.

"You are such a cutie," I affectionately said to her. We laughed together all the time.

I commented, "Your hair looks great!"

"Oh, do you like it, I straightened it," she blushed.

I watched TV for quite a while and heard knocks on the walls. I knew it was the pipes. The toilet flushed twice by itself then kept running, I jiggled the handle and it stopped. I'm sure there was a problem with the plumbing. I heard a gentle wind coming from under the adjoining door. I knew it was probably because of an opened window. I prayed and thought of my dear friend, but I took back my wish of hoping to be visited by her.

I woke up the next morning thinking of her in that room. We had an early sign-in for our flight to Miami. I wanted to go down early to talk to the security guard, so I quickly showered and threw on my uniform.

I asked the bellman if he was there when they found Rebecca. He said, "No, but the security guard over there is the one who found her." I walked in the direction to where he was pointing.

"Hi, my name is Chris, and I would like to talk to you about my friend, the girl you found in her room. Do you feel comfortable with that?" I could tell he was very saddened and deeply affected by her death.

He said, "Sure. Another flight attendant and I were the ones who found her. She was in her uniform; it must have happened soon after she entered the room. The bed was made and the curtains were still open. Nothing in the bathroom had been touched."

The speculations were brain aneurysm or something heart related. She was found lying on the bed with her feet still on the floor.

When I flew with her three months earlier, I had asked, "Rebecca, you have fair skin like me, do you have any issues with skin cancer?" I don't remember exactly what she said now but we talked about our health and I am sure she would have mentioned any serious conditions.

When our crew arrived at the airport, Terry and I wanted to try and identity the flight attendant who, along with the security guard, had found Rebecca. We knew it was a male flight attendant. We pulled up the information on the computer and saw it was our good friend Randy. We called him to see how he was doing. He said the days are okay, but her face haunts him at night. Randy told us his version of what happened.

"After the crew signed in for their rooms at the hotel, they were all supposed to eat dinner together. Rebecca was the one who initiated the dinner plans. She didn't look sick or have any symptoms that might have signaled to the crew something was wrong. Suzie said she was tired, so she wasn't going to join them."

For security reasons, when we enter our rooms we sometimes leave the door open (propped by our suitcase) to make sure everything is safe inside. Rebecca already closed her door that day.

Randy continued, "Suzie knocked on her door to check on her, but heard no response. She assumed Rebecca was probably talking on the phone or was in the bathroom. Cindy, the other flight attendant and I, were waiting for Rebecca to join us for dinner that night. She never showed up. I called her room, but there was no answer. We thought maybe she was making some phone calls or just too tired and changed her mind."

Had Suzie been to dinner, she probably would have thought something was wrong because she had knocked on the door earlier and there was no answer. The next morning for pick-up, Rebecca was not there. He and the security guard went to Rebecca's room and found her lying on the bed. He said he shook her repeatedly yelling out her name.

A few months later, Rebecca's best friend Dawn and I were flying to the same destination on our days off.

We grieved at the loss of our sweet friend and I shared the few details I had learned of her passing. We loved her dearly. Rebecca and Dawn were in the same training class twenty-three years earlier and had remained best friends throughout their career. My heart went out to her.

I asked, "Was it a brain aneurism like everyone said?"

"No," she said. "It was called 'cardiac insufficiency.' She didn't have enough oxygen going to her heart."

The doctor said had she been aware of her condition it could have easily been treated. He said Rebecca may have even experienced some mild heart attacks prior to her passing. She had been taking an arthritis medication for a year. Scar tissue had built up around her heart.

I still grieve and my heart goes out to everyone who loved her — especially her son.

We miss you, Rebecca.

51

No Liquids

A couple of years after 9/11, I had a terrifying dream of airplanes exploding in midair. After each explosion, I gasped. I woke my husband and shared my horrific nightmare.

Shortly after that, I was on a three-day trip. The first night we arrived in Minneapolis at 12:30 a.m. Our pickup time the next morning was 10:30. I thought maybe I could sleep in, but my internal clock woke me up around 6 a.m. EST.

I made my coffee, jumped back into bed and turned on the TV. Ever since the terrorist attacks, I dreaded the phrase "breaking news." On this day, there it was in bold letters — and once again it was about terrorists and airplanes. I felt my hair stand up on my arm. *Not again*! British authorities arrested 24 people who had conspired to blow up as many as ten U.S. bound aircraft using liquid explosives hidden in carry-on luggage. *This was exactly my dream.* I was glued to the TV as the Homeland Security Advisory System escalated to its highest level, red, signaling imminent attack. Since I was leaving later that morning, I wondered what the day would bring.

The van ride to the airport was surprisingly quiet. I think we were all somewhat in disbelief and recalling that awful day in 2001. It was clear that the terrorists were still targeting airplanes.

As we entered the airport, a sea of frustrated passengers snaked their way slowly up to security check points. The ban on liquids was in effect and the same scenario was playing out in airports all over the United States and in the U.K. As our bags hit the conveyer belt, the TSA officer said to the screener, "It's the crew, it's the crew, let them through," in an effort to speed up processing. I saw container after container of liquids that were now considered a threat.

The gate agent later told us the earlier flight crews had major problems going through security. No one was prepared for the new rules. Crew and passengers alike were being directed to toss all liquids from hair sprays, mouthwash, after-shave, all drinks including water bottles as well as their precious Starbucks coffee. It was all going right in the trash and it was chaos.

I heard many stories of frustrated passengers as they boarded our flight. One lady complained, "The screeners took my expensive perfume." Another lost her favorite nail polish. I empathized with them, but assured them security was just doing their jobs under the circumstances.

I was glad for that day to be over. As we passed by security on our way out of the airport, I saw two huge garbage cans filled with toiletries. *What are they going to do with all that stuff?*

The next morning I turned on the television hoping not to see breaking news. I was relieved that nothing happened overnight and the security level was lowered to yellow.

A couple of weeks later, I took my mom and dad to Cancun. I hadn't gone through security as a passenger yet, so I, too, became a victim of the liquid ban. I lost my hair spray, lip gloss and even a sealed container of applesauce. I appreciated the crew exemption even more and felt for all the passengers trying to conform to the new restrictions.

It is somewhat frustrating that even when we successfully foil terrorist plans to kill innocent people, they still violate our liberty. Richard Reid's infamous attempt to blow up his shoe on his flight has resulted in the removal of our footwear when we pass through security. The terrorist who tried to ignite his underwear helped drive the adoption of full visual body image screening at airport security checkpoints.

All in all, the entire London plot and the ban on liquids was just a reminder that they are still out there. We must stay vigilant and if anything looks suspicious on the airplane, don't hesitate to tell a flight attendant.

52

PMS

*H*ormones! Sometimes they come in handy. "Oh, I must be PMS-ing." They can also be a hindrance. "Oh, you must be PMS-ing."

My cycle is pretty regular. Eight days before, I feel a little irritable. Small things are big things. The grocery cart sticks, and I get ticked off. The person who pulls out in front of me gets the look. My poor husband can do no right. I am panicked and burdened, but can't pinpoint why.

Six days before the cycle, I am very emotional. I feel all choked up when one of my favorite songs comes on the radio. Sad commercials make me cry. I look at my husband admiringly. Can you imagine the conflict of emotions he must feel at that time? That's why he says, "You're not the only one who goes through PMS." It really does a number on him, too. This is also not a good time for me to make important decisions as I am a little non-decisive.

Then, four days before, I am the bottomless pit. I eat whatever I can get my hands on, preferably something salty and sweet. Grocery shopping at this time is not a good idea. I eat a meal and an hour later, I am looking for something else to eat.

Two days before, I get the pooch. My stomach extends out like I am two months pregnant. Nothing fits right, and I kick myself for eating so much. I assure myself I am just retaining water.

One day before, my complexion is pasty and gaunt. My eyes look dull. I also tend to feel insecure. I want to be left alone. This is, of course, very difficult when you have to fly for a living and are constantly surrounded by people.

My words are all messed up and my mind is foggy.

"Honey, would you like some 'Guatemala' with your quesadilla?"

"Yes," he laughs, "I will have some 'Guatemala'."

Not all women go through this, but those who do will identify (so will their partner).

On one particular flight, around day seven or eight before the cycle, I was just plain irritable! Working the first class cabin was not going to be easy. After everyone boarded, the agent closed the aircraft door. The two flight attendants in the back of the aircraft came rushing to me. "We've got a problem in the coach cabin; this man won't take his seat. He is sitting in a middle seat and is demanding an aisle. We are completely full." I told the shaken flight attendants not to worry; I would handle him.

Back I went, ready for a battle. He was standing halfway through the cabin with his arms crossed also ready for battle.

I asked him, "What seems to be the problem here, sir?"

"I've paid for this ticket months in advance; I am not going to sit in a middle seat!" he yelled.

I looked at him with a pleasant but don't-mess-with-me look and stated, "You have two choices here. We are completely full. You can either sit down now or take the next flight. What do you want to do, sir?"

He saw that I meant business, rolled his eyes like a spoiled little boy but sat down in his seat. He was complacent for the rest of the flight.

Another time, around day six before the cycle, I was completely emotional. I was outside the terminal pulling tickets for our flight. This particular city had a military base. I noticed a group of military personnel dressed in their fatigues. I asked one of them where they were going. "Desert storm," he said. I gulped.

There were several boys with their families. They waited until the very last minute to board the aircraft. I watched as their fathers, mothers, wives, and children said goodbye to them not knowing if it might be the last time they would ever see them again. Every time I heard a wail, my eyes filled with tears. I tried not to look at them, but I couldn't help it. Finally, I could not contain my tears any more. I kept wiping drops off my cheek until the kind agent came over with a tissue. I thanked him.

The agent walked over to the families and said it was time to go. I hesitantly took the boys' tickets while trying to hide my emotions. The families asked if I would take care of their loved ones on board. Tears welled up again. "I will," I promised.

One day, on a day or two before the cycle, I was feeling like I needed to be left alone. Unfortunately, I was flying that day. I parked my car in the employee lot and took the bus to the airport. I did not want to go. Hesitantly, after entering the airport, I looked at the monitor to see where my flight was leaving. My body felt heavy as I moved. Slowly, I proceeded feeling sorry for myself the whole way to the gate. My airplane just arrived and all the passengers were still deplaning.

I walked over to the agent who was carrying a list of gate connections. Agents and flight attendants are peers; one has no authority over the other. I don't know why, but in my PMS haze I asked her permission on where I sat.

"Would you mind if I wait for the passengers to get off the aircraft, in those chairs over there? I'd rather not be around people as long as I can," I chuckled.

She looked at me condescendingly, "I don't care what you do!" she snapped. My PMS was absolutely furious. *What an evil person*!

I sat in a row of chairs away from the public eye, kicking myself for being such a wimp. Thank God my phone rang to break up my self-loathing. It was my mom. The passengers were now off the aircraft, so I casually headed down the jet bridge while talking to her. I smiled at the flight attendants who were getting off the airplane. A few seconds later, the same flight attendants were trying to get my attention. Behind them was that nasty gate agent screaming at me. *I had just about enough of her.*

I said, "Hold on, Mom." I yelled right back at the agent in full PMS fury. "What, what do you want?" Apparently, she was taken aback by my aggressiveness.

"You can't go on the aircraft; the cabin service will be cleaning soon," she sniped.

"Excuse me, but I have been flying for a long time and I think I know what I can and cannot do," I retorted.

The agent huffed, but backed down. I stepped on the airplane satisfied I regained my power.

My poor mom was still on the phone listening to the conversation. I'm sure she was horrified at her sweet daughter's behavior. She has seen me that way only a couple of times. She always responds by saying, "That's just the Leo in you." It might be, but I always blame it on "PMS."

53

Just Shake It

$\mathscr{I}$t was the final leg of yet another brutal day with a completely full flight from Dallas/Ft. Worth to Fort Lauderdale. Needless to say the flight attendants were a little spent. The only good part about this leg was, we were going home.

As our boarding process began, I saw a uniformed crew member making her way through coach. When she approached me in the back galley, she introduced herself and stated the airplane was full and she would be taking a jumpseat. When we are non-reving (the employee benefit of flying for free) and the airplane is full of passengers, an unpleasant option is to ride on the jumpseat. This is a really great benefit when we are trying to get somewhere, but we all know the working flight attendants would rather we not be there. We have a limited amount of space to work in the galley and the last thing we need is an extra body.

As I was busy crushing the ice, the flight attendant exited the restroom. "The toilet doesn't have any water coming down when you flush it," she said. "You need to tell the captain to call maintenance."

I thought about it for a second. I have been flying for a long time and I know what happens when you call maintenance. A delay is somewhat inevitable. Because we were going home and it was the last flight of the night, I didn't want to be delayed for a restroom that doesn't flush. After all, being on a 757, there was a restroom just behind first class the coach cabin could use along with the other one in the back.

"Listen, if it was a safety related issue, I would not hesitate to call, or if it was a longer flight I would take immediate action, but a restroom on a two and a half hour flight?"

She looked at her watch and said sarcastically, "We do have twenty five minutes before departure."

I grabbed the phone against my better judgment and called the captain. "We have a non-safety issue that really isn't a big deal, but if maintenance could check to see if our toilet can be fixed easily, we would appreciate it. But, we don't want to take a delay."

Ten minutes before departure, we saw the mechanic heading our way. While explaining the situation I again stated, "If it is not an easy fix, we don't want to be delayed; they can take care of it in Fort Lauderdale."

He walked in the restroom, flushed the toilet two or three times and came out. "Nope, it's not working; we'll have to placard it." This simply means it is out of service and will be taken care of at the next station. I knew I should have trusted my instincts because it took another twenty minutes for the paper to be filled out. Now, we were officially delayed.

Meanwhile, the first class flight attendant came to the back galley to see what was going on. I took no blame and pointed my finger at the non-revving flight attendant in a joking way and said, "She made me call." They both agreed it was a bad idea, and I'm sure everyone learned something that night.

After about an hour into the flight and everyone's beverage was taking effect, the line to the restroom was getting rather long. I directed some passengers to use the restroom behind first class and noticed several men waiting in line still in coach. I explained to the first male passenger that the out of order toilet would not flush.

I looked at him directly in the eye and said delicately, "If you don't use any paper, you can still use that toilet."

He said, "What you're saying is, as long as I just give it a jiggle, we're good to go."

"That's right," I laughed.

He looked at me in a flirting way and said, "I think we have just bonded."

All the other male passengers in line heard the exchange and that was the start of one crass joke after another! The "wiener" went to the young man who entered the lav singing KC and the Sunshine Band's song, "shake, shake, shake… shake, shake, shake… shake your booty."

54

FAA

The Federal Aviation Administration sets all the safety guidelines for every airline. In other words, they rule! Whatever they say, goes. Whether it is the aircraft specifications, the cabin regulations or the seat your child sits in, they have to be monitored and approved by the FAA. I certainly feel safer to fly, knowing they have established the best safety guidelines and procedures.

The pilots and flight attendants can get "check rides" from an FAA inspector to make sure we are doing our jobs correctly. If the inspector is checking the cabin crew, he first wants to see that our manuals are up to date. Our manuals are our flying "Bibles," and we must have them with us at all times. Our company provides us with current revisions and bulletins that must be inserted by a certain date. If we are inspected and either a bulletin or revision is not in our manuals, we can get slapped with a personal fine. The inspector also checks to see if we are complying with safety regulations. This includes verifying that we conduct a passenger seatbelt check, locate the emergency equipment, brief our exit row passengers in case of an emergency and clear the bulkhead and exit rows of any luggage on the floor. He or she can also test our knowledge of emergency situations.

Virginia, a fellow flight attendant, told me her story. A male FAA inspector was on their 757 aircraft to give them a check ride. The inspector stood next to her behind the last row of first class for the boarding process. Two ladies were sitting on the left side (9BC) and two ladies were sitting on the right side of the exit row (9DE). As the women settled into their seats, Virginia saw they left some of their belongings in front of them. Virginia reminded them that they were in an exit row, and everything had to go in the overhead bin for takeoff and landing. She advised them to do so before the overhead bins were full.

The right row complied, but the ladies on the left side still had their purses lying on the floor. Once again, Virginia stated that everything needed to go in the overhead bin. All the passengers boarded, so Virginia closed the overhead compartments. The FAA inspector took his seat in the forward part of coach.

When the flight attendants walk through the cabin to do their safety compliance checks, they are looking for three major things:

One is that your seatbelt is fastened. When we check seatbelts, we are looking for the obvious; that everyone has one on. An overweight individual may be too embarrassed to ask for an extension or there might be a mother who has her seatbelt fastened around her and her child. The seatbelt should be fastened only around the mother with the baby held tightly in her lap. If an aborted takeoff occurred, for example, and the brakes were hit hard, the child could suffer internal injuries from the seatbelt.

The second is that your seatback is upright. I have seen several comedy potshots about the seatback issue. Does it really make a difference if your seat is back a few inches? If you are in an emergency evacuation and the person behind you is trying to get out of his row, it makes a big difference. The same goes for the tray table down. If you are in an emergency evacuation and your tray table is not up, it could prevent you as well as the person next to you from getting out in a timely manner.

The third thing is making sure the luggage is not blocking the exit row, and not lying on the floor in a bulkhead. The main reason for this is because there have been some emergencies where anything on the floor was basically a flying torpedo.

When Virginia was doing her compliance checks, she noticed that 9BC still had their purses on the floor. She went over to direct them once again. This time the FAA inspector rose from his seat and appeared next to her. "Excuse me, ladies," he said in his intimidating voice. "Which part of what Virginia asked of you did you not understand?" He asked them for their name and address and gave them each a personal fine. He continued, "If Virginia had not asked you to put your belongings up, she would be getting the fine." *Yikes!*

I have had several inspectors on my flights throughout my career. When word spreads that they will be checking us, the flights attendants scramble to the back of the aircraft making sure our manuals match everyone else's and are up to date. They're not there to make trouble for us; they just want to make sure we're in compliance.

On one particular flight, we were on our last segment of a four-leg day that terminated in Nashville. Most of the time when the plane is not full, the agents leave the last row available so the flight attendants can have a place to rest after the service and keep an eye on the cabin. We usually place our bags on the seats to let the passengers know they are taken. After all, we need some pampering whenever we can get it. The only problem on this flight was that I left my bags on the seat for takeoff and landing, which is a no-no.

Cynthia and I did our beverage service in coach. After picking up the cabin, I collapsed on the last row aisle seat. In the other row adjacent to me was a mechanic who worked for us. I quietly shared with him my story about the light fuse that was smoking on my flight. I wanted to get his opinion.

Little did I know, the man sitting in front of me was actually with the FAA. The captain said to prepare the cabin for landing. Cynthia and I picked up the cabin and did our safety checks. She did what she was supposed to do and took her jumpseat. I, on the other hand, wasn't finished with my story. I continued until I heard the landing gear. I told the mechanic I would be right back.

So I sat on my jumpseat just before the wheels hit the tarmac. I gave the aircraft a little time to do some maneuvering on the runway and then ran back to finish my story, leaving my exit basically unmanned. It was still close to me, but I am not supposed to get out of my jumpseat.

When I finished my story, I sat down on the jumpseat again. The captain said, "Flight attendants, prepare for arrival." I disarmed my door and went back to the last row. Everyone deplaned the aircraft except for one passenger. It was the man sitting in front of me.

He said, "Ladies, I need to have a word with you." He took something out of his pocket and snapped it to reveal his FAA badge.

I looked at Cynthia and saw the color drain from her face.

"I'm with the FAA," he said. He looked me in the eye and pointed to the last row.

"Are your bags supposed to be there for takeoff and landing?"

Then he turned to Cynthia and asked, "Are your bags supposed to be under the seat blocking the emergency equipment?"

We didn't defend ourselves because we knew we were busted. I wrinkled my nose and shook my head no. Cynthia did the same. He said he wanted to make sure we knew they were out there watching us. It took poor Cynthia a day or so to recover from that one. I was lucky and grateful he didn't fine me for getting out of my jumpseat.

55

Code Red

*O*ur last day of our 3-day trip was a doozy; Philadelphia to Miami, Miami to Washington, and Washington to Miami.

We had a very early pickup from our hotel that morning, sign-in by 6 a.m. taking off around 7 a.m. Laura and I were working in the coach cabin on a full 737 aircraft with 144 passengers.

After reaching a safe cruising altitude, we took the cart out in the aisle to complete our beverage service. At row 18, a female passenger had her leg halfway out in the aisle.

"Ma'am, you need to move your leg, ma'am. Wake up, ma'am, we need to get by," both Laura and I chimed. There was no response. Laura was the one facing her and realized something was wrong.

"Are you okay?" she questioned.

Again, there was no response. She was unconscious.

We heard a voice a few rows back, "Mom?" Three of her daughters were traveling with her, along with her best friend.

They were anticipating going on a fun filled Caribbean cruise. "I am a nurse," said one of the daughters.

Laura and I quickly pushed the cart back to the galley. We obtained the oxygen from the overhead bin. The woman was unconscious but breathing. Our procedure is to give her oxygen. I ran to the number one flight attendant and said the words that none of us ever want to hear on an airplane: "We have a possible code red."

Code red is a signal to get the defibrillator, medical kit, and the bag that contains the mask and gloves for CPR. A defibrillator or AED is a piece of emergency equipment that can monitor the heart thru padded sensors. If the patient has no pulse, the monitor may advise you to shock the person or to start CPR.

The number one flight attendant called the captain to let him know the condition of the passenger. She also made a PA announcement asking if we had a doctor or medical personnel on board.

There was one passenger call light that went on. I was getting the medical equipment, so Laura got the light. We already had the oxygen on the passenger. A doctor, along with the patient's daughter, were our official helpers. We had a nurse technician sitting in the same row as the patient. She was actually more of a hindrance than a help.

The doctor asked for a stethoscope and blood pressure cuff.

The nurse technician kept yelling, "Get the AED on her, get the AED on her."

I finally said to her, "Ma'am, we have been trained for emergencies and are following our procedures. We have the AED and all medical equipment right here if necessary."

The patient's daughters said she has fainted before, but this didn't seem like a fainting spell. She wasn't coming out of consciousness. The captain said he didn't want to take any chances with the passenger, so he made a wise decision to divert to Raleigh and take her off the aircraft.

After a while, she started to fade in and out of consciousness. I put a cloth with ice on her forehead and turned the vents on for air. She took off her mask and mumbled she wanted to lie down.

The heckler in the background shouted again, "Get the AED on her."

Then I thought, *Please don't die on me, I don't want to be haunted by that nurse technician's voice.* With everyone in agreement, we decided to lie her down and go ahead and monitor her with the AED. This was easier said than done.

I looked at the patient who was close to 200 pounds. Our procedures are to lift up the armrest and roll the patient to the floor. I discreetly tried to find the release button for the armrest, but couldn't find it. On some aircrafts the armrest doesn't lift, so I figured this was one of those. My next move was to lift her up from her seat to maneuver her to the aisle. I had two assistants help me from behind, but most of her weight was on me. I positioned my arms under her arms. She was so clammy! I slowly lifted her up. She was conscious enough at that point to listen to my commands.

"Walk to your right," I said. She obediently took baby steps to the right. She wouldn't lie down.

I told her, "Bend your knees so you can lie down, honey." She obeyed, and all three of us lowered her to the floor.

As she was being lowered, her oxygen mask was still on. The oxygen tube just like a luggage strap got caught on the armrest. "The oxygen!" someone yelled. I quickly took the tank from under the seat and gave it to Laura. She put the tank under the seat closest to the passenger's head.

Laura was at the head of the patient, and I knelt at her legs. The nurse handed me the AED. Our procedure for using the defibrillator is to use it on a bare chest. I looked at this woman's huge breasts. *This was not good.* The instructors told us in training to do what it takes to get the shirt off even if scissors are required. Now, this wasn't a life or death situation, so I wasn't sure what to do. She was wearing a button down blouse, but the bra was going to be a problem. I mentioned to Laura something about scissors, and my favorite bystander yelled out, "You don't need scissors!" Actually, I was grateful for that comment because I didn't know you could put the pads on under the bra.

We positioned her shirt trying to avoid exposing too much of her. I took the pads and gave one to Laura. I put one on where the heart is. Laura took the other one and laid it down on her clavicle. The AED kept saying, "Apply pads, apply pads," I repositioned each pad and it worked. The machine said, "Monitoring the patient, do not touch the patient."

I glanced outside and saw we were close to landing. I told our assistants we need to take our jumpseats for landing and to ring the flight attendant call button if you need anything. Our procedures are to get the patient out of the aisle for landing in case we have an emergency. Due to the time restriction and situation, that wasn't going to happen. Sometimes you have to use your own common sense and judgment. I was grateful she was staying with us.

The paramedics were there to meet the flight in Raleigh and placed her on a gurney. Her best friend stayed with her. I believe that in denial the daughters continued on to Miami thinking their mother would take the next flight.

All in all, we did a pretty good job under stressful circum-stances. I was relieved to practice applying the pads to a living, breathing person as opposed to someone who might have already expired!

My next trip was to Las Vegas and was working the coach cabin. I shared with a colleague my story of the code red passenger and about having the fire extinguishers out in the aisles the month before. She said, "You know what, I don't think I want to fly with you this month." We both laughed. Just at that moment, the flight attendant call lights chimed simultaneously. Kim and I glanced at each other in disbelief for a second and ran to see what the commotion was about.

A young, attractive female was thrashing furiously against the seats. She was having a seizure. Our procedure for a seizure is to cushion the area with blankets until the passenger is stabilized. Our number one flight attendant was also a nurse, and we had two doctors who immediately offered their assistance. All I had to do for this emergency was to provide the blankets and make sure she had plenty of OJ. That was a piece of cake.

Later on, Kim jokingly proclaimed it was all my fault. I do seem to have a lot of experiences other flight attendants don't have.

56

Changes Over the Years

$\mathscr{W}$e have witnessed significant changes in the airline industry and as a result, the flying experience is not the same for passengers and crew alike. Some of the changes have been needed and had a positive influence on air travel. Other changes are not quite as popular, making us long for the good old days.

When I began my career in 1986, mobile computing did not even exist, at least at our airline. None of our procedures were automated. The flight attendants checked in before their flight by signing their name on a clip board. Now everything we do is digitized. Computers streamlined everything and made the life of crewmembers and our airline much easier. We sign-in for our trips on the computer an hour before our flight. If for some reason we do not sign-in, the crew scheduler is immediately alerted to call in a standby flight attendant.

The internet's effect on the airline industry cannot be overstated. Airline websites automate processes from ticketing to seating. Remember when you had to call a travel agency to find out the cost of airfare! Hello Expedia, Kayak, Priceline etc.

I also remember using ramp stands, such as the one the president still uses coming off Air Force One today. Thank goodness someone invented the jet bridge (the contraption that lets you get from the airport terminal directly to the airplane without having to walk outside and up the stairs).

On one of my trips using the archaic ramp stand in Aruba, the captain made a special announcement to hold on to your hats while getting off the aircraft, "It's mighty windy out there." As everyone was deplaning, the captain and I noticed a man wearing a toupee heading down the aisle. We said "Uh-oh" together as we watched him take his first step onto the ramp stand. Sure enough his toupee flew straight up in the air. Both of his hands were occupied with his luggage, so he had to wait till he reached the bottom of the stairs to retrieve his masculinity and his dignity. Kudos for jet bridges!

Remember the wheelies? Those were steel contraptions with gigantic wheels attached to them. We strapped our suit-cases onto them instead of carrying our luggage. Then some genius put wheels on the luggage and added a convenient pop up handle. From what I understand it was actually a pilot and a flight attendant who came up with the idea. It took quite a while for the macho pilots and male flight attendants to get used to wheeling their suitcase around. They wouldn't even use the steel wheelies; they insisted on carrying their luggage "like real men." Eventually, they gave in to the idea and now everyone has suitcases with wheels. In fact, the flight attendants and passengers now all have the same bags.

While deplaning in Philadelphia, an elderly passenger took my bag from the overhead bin by mistake. After everyone deplaned the aircraft, the other flight attendant working with me noticed the suitcase in the overhead bin did not look like mine.

I looked up and said, "It's not."

I ran to the gate agents with the passenger's suitcase. The agents had fifteen minutes before boarding passengers for the next flight. "I hate to tell you this, but my manual is in my bag and that is a "no-go" item," I said. "We have to find the passenger who mistakenly took my bag or this plane isn't going anywhere." We searched the passenger's luggage left behind and found a name on a prescription bottle. After paging his name several times, he returned to the gate with my bag. Since then, I have ribbons on my suitcase for identification.

Some of you may agree or disagree with this ban: no smoking on the airplane. In the old days, as the plane took off, the passengers in the last five rows in coach waited with anticipation, cigarettes in hand, until the no smoking sign went off. Then, practically in unison, twenty five to thirty passengers lit up. The flight attendants were trapped on the back jump-seat inhaling everyone's second hand smoke. Many of the smokers booked their seat in the non-smoking zone, so they didn't have to sit in the smoking area. When they felt like lighting up, they stood or took an empty seat to smoke. Of all the changes implemented, I think this is one I appreciate the most.

On a flight heading to Las Vegas, a lady sitting next to a window, who obviously had too much to drink, stopped me and slurring her words said, "Es-cuuse me, I think I may have dropped my cigarette." I hurriedly cleared the row of passengers and found the smoking cigarette on the floor. Think of how dangerous that was; a lit cigarette on the carpet of an oxygenated airplane flying at 33,000 feet.

No discussion of changes would be complete without acknowledging how much cell phones have impacted our lives. I remember waiting in line to use the public telephone in the airport only to pick it up and find a horrible aftershave smell. Sometimes you could smell the stench of someone's bad breath lingering on the mouthpiece. Who knew that twenty years from then, public telephones would become virtually obsolete? I am sure none of us who routinely travel can overstate the convenience and connectedness that cell phones have provided. I can't imagine life without them.

Of course, there is always the bad with the good. There are the annoying loud talkers and those who simply won't stop talking. We all stand by politely but uncomfortably participating in a conversation we neither wanted nor have any business hearing. I do think it's great that you can use cell phones on the ground, but I am totally against using cell phones in the air. Can you imagine sleeping and someone's cell phone rings next to you? As phones have become smart we use them for all kinds of applications. I remember the first time I saw someone with a wireless ear piece, I thought there was a crazy person loose in the terminal. Now, it's no big deal. It's funny how you just get used to things.

One of the biggest changes on the airplane is of course the quality of the food; that is, if you have any at all. I used to serve strawberry blintzes or cheddar cheese omelets in first class. In coach, we always served pancakes or omelets for break-fast. Even if the flight was only an hour and a half, we would bust our butts to get that food out and picked up. For lunch we always had something warm to serve. Perhaps a burrito or a hot turkey sandwich was the choice of the day. For dinner we served our world famous chicken or beef. A hundred and twenty or so times down the aisle asking, "Chicken or beef, chicken or beef?"

When I first started working international flights, we were serving beef or shrimp. I knew beef in Spanish was called carne but I didn't know how to say shrimp. I asked the male Spanish speaking flight attendant working with me how to say shrimp in Spanish. He said to say "cojones." The first few rows I asked the Spanish speaking passengers if they wanted carne or cojones. They looked at me funny, so I showed them the food. A few times they just laughed at me. I glanced up at the other flight attendant in frustration. He was laughing hysterically. Cojones is Spanish for testicles. Camarones is shrimp. I was asking the passengers if they wanted beef or balls!

For a late night flight, we served something light. We fondly called it the hockey puck. It was a little round roll with a piece of meat and lettuce in it, served with a sweet pickle. Sometimes the bread got pretty hard: I guess that's how they got their name.

On really short flights we handed out salted or honey-roasted peanuts. Over the years though, allergies to nuts became more common. We realized people could actually die from simply being exposed to them, so perhaps we became hyper vigilant. However, I think the possible liability became too much of an issue and there went our peanuts.

The hot food for breakfast and lunch was starting to phase out in the coach cabin on domestic flights. The food service industry thought of a new type of service called a bistro bag. Before you boarded, a huge bin full of bags was placed on the jet bridge. You simply picked one up if you wanted something to eat. It was like having a picnic in the sky. I thought this was a great idea until everyone kept handing the flight attendants empty bags throughout the whole flight. At least with trays, you had one pickup service and that was it.

Then 9/11 happened. The ripple effect hit everyone hard. Severe cutbacks were made just to keep the airline afloat. Food was one of those cutbacks. The heavy ovens were taken off in coach on many of our aircraft to save on fuel. The days of warm food on domestic flights were over. People would ask, "Isn't it easier for you not to serve food?" In a way it is, but in a way it isn't. The flight attendants have to put up with disgruntled passengers who inevitably ask, "Isn't there anything to eat?" Also, the flight attendants have to bring their own food to work. This means we take the time on our day off to plan and prepare what we are going to eat for the next couple of days. We started a new service called "buy on board". If you want to eat, you have to pay for it. I guess something is better than nothing.

The impact of 9/11 also resulted in our passengers losing many familiar luxuries. Our magazine racks are now empty, and the first class newspapers are a thing of the past. This next one really hurt me, as you know, I love kids and we used to pass out toy airplane wings to the children, but they too have gone. Our airline's initials on our coffee stir sticks have become generic. We get catered milk only on morning flights. Sometimes the flight attendants are able to save some milk on ice so the passengers in the afternoon can have some milk with their coffee instead of the powdered cream packets. The pillows and blankets on domestic flights are gone. The most unpopular change in airline travel is paying extra for practically everything.

There used to be a lot more love affairs that started in the air. It was more glamorous and exciting in those days. Most of the pilots and flight attendants were hired in their early 20s and 30s. As soon as a female flight attendant walked on the airplane, the pilots in the cockpit craned their necks to check them out. We were like candies in a jar. Which one would be the flavor of the day? Now most of the "candies" have either hardened or turned soft in the middle. Many of us are now married and have a life at home. Sometimes we don't even see the pilots until we leave the aircraft and say a quick, "Oh, hi

I'm Chris." The hours spent flirting in the cockpit have been replaced by looking at a magazine on our down time.

Back in the day it was a privilege to fly. Passengers dressed up as if they were going out for an evening of fine dining. Little girls wore their frilly dresses, and little boys had on a suit and tie. When the airline employees traveled non-revenue, (standby) we were required to follow a strict dress code or we could be denied boarding. Now, we see it all. Sweat suits, flip flops and tank tops are now the norm. Girls wear tops that expose half of their breasts and guys wear shorts that expose half of their butts. Our airline actually had to lower our standby dress regulations because we stood out so much when we traveled.

One thing that hasn't changed is the restroom on the airplane. Think about it, on a jet is about the only time you won't see a women's or men's sign on the restroom door. It's kind of funny that in restaurants, gas stations, or in stores you wouldn't think of using the restroom of the opposite sex. The women usually wait forever in line while the men quickly come in and out of the men's restroom. When you are on the airplane, you don't think twice about going in after the opposite sex has come out. Now the men know what it is like to wait and wait and wait.

The more people fly, the more they adapt to change. I see more and more pillows and blankets brought on by passengers.

They know if they don't bring their own food, they may not eat.

Change is fearful, but given time we all seem to adapt. All and all, flying is still the best way to get from point A to point B. I still look out the window in amazement. *How can this big tube stay up in the air?*

With all the many changes that have occurred in the airline industry, I still enjoy my job. I want every passenger's trip to be a good one. Flight attendants tell me they can see that I am from the old school. I believe in working hard, and sometimes you have to smile when you don't feel like it. My momma always said, "It's okay to be in a bad mood, but it's not okay to take it out on someone else."

57

Dimes Everywhere

My grandmother and I shared a deep, spiritual conversation a year before she died. After my grandfather passed away of a heart attack in the bedroom, his spirit lingered around their house for about six months. She occasionally smelled his Old Spice aftershave, heard knocks under the couch and his workshop light would come on in the evening along with other friendly hauntings. I told her, "Grandma, I always find dimes, hundreds of them."

"You know Christi, it is supposed to be a sign of something," she said. I knew that, but what?

Generally, I find one on every trip. I keep a special treasure chest in my closet especially for them. Some flight attendants even associate me with dimes. I can't explain where they come from, but every time I find one, I say thank you. The most I have ever found in one day was six, four on the airplane and two in the airport. My most unusual find was in the mountains of New Hampshire. I was squatting to take a potty break and there in the middle of nowhere, lay a bright shiny dime. My husband flipped out on that one.

Sometime later I did find one possible explanation. A flight attendant was on my flight commuting to work from Dallas to West Palm Beach. The last row was empty, so she came back to visit. It was a night-time flight with a light load.

After finishing the passengers' beverage service, I sat next to her for a chat. As women do, we conversed on a variety of topics — one of which was her admission she could see spirits even as a young girl. I told her I have some kind of sixth sense and she said, "I know." She went on to say that she predicted an airplane crash in detail. She wrote it all down before it happened. We shared a few more stories and eventually moved on to everyday topics.

She then looked above me and with a slight cocking of her head said, "There is a spirit with you."

"What?" I said. *Can you imagine someone telling you that?*

"He is right above you," she said.

I stammered and asked, "Is, is that good?"

"He is taller than you and has broad shoulders," she continued.

I told her my brother-in-law passed away only the weekend before. "Is it him?"

"No, he tells me he has been with you for a long time."

She told me his head tilted back slightly as he chuckled. *I got that; I must be quite the character for him to follow around.*

"You have placed yourself in a lot of danger, and he has been there to protect you."

That is true! Now all that would have been fine to hear, but she continued.

"He wants me to tell you that he is there for you."

I said, "Okay."

"Tough times are ahead and he wants you to know you are not alone," she said.

My heart sank! "I have had a lot of skin cancer."

"No, not you, a loved one," she said.

That, of course, freaked me out!

I went home and immediately searched the internet for guardian angels. There is an ample supply of information. One article said they are messengers from God given to each child at birth.

I also read that they can be your inner voice. I remembered all the times when I must have set my alarm clock wrong, but woke up exactly when I was supposed to anyway. It was like someone was nudging me to get up.

The last and final thing that I read was they can leave you coins to let you know they are there with you. Bingo! Maybe that is where all the dimes come from.

It has been several years since that conversation. I do sense a guardian angel in my life, or at least a spiritual presence that does guide and influence me. That exchange in the back of the aircraft was one of the most memorable encounters I have ever had.

58

Emergency Chimes!

*A*pril 2, 2008. It was a nice day to fly. The weather the day before had been pretty awful. We were relieved when the captain said there was going to be no weather problems from Dallas to Memphis.

Our day would be a long one. We started in San Antonio with a 5 a.m. sign-in. Our first leg was going to Dallas. Then, a Memphis turn back to Dallas. The last leg would take us home to West Palm Beach.

The flight to Memphis was one we were looking forward to because we were scheduled for only 35 passengers. *What an easy flight this was going to be.*

After take-off, I took full advantage of the light load. I scrambled to an empty passenger's seat to get comfortable. After all, no one was sitting in the back of the airplane except for a young woman who was fast asleep.

As I peacefully opened my magazine, the unthinkable happened. The first time in my career where I actually heard it: the signal notifying us that we have an emergency! I immediately ran to the phone next to my jumpseat. "This is Chris," I said trying to not sound panicked. I heard Colleen say she was on the phone too.

"Hey guys," the captain said. "We have a problem with our hydraulics."

The other flight attendant, Bradley, asked what was going on. I pointed to his phone firmly. He quickly retrieved his phone so we all were listening.

The captain continued, "There is no fluid in the right hand hydraulics. We don't know where it went, but we are going back to Dallas."

I went completely white. I know one word you do not want to hear in an emergency and that is the word "hydraulics." You need hydraulics to maneuver and land the airplane.

I looked at the passenger who was previously sleeping so soundly. She was wide awake now.

Seeing that she knowingly seemed very interested, I mouthed to her, "Are you a flight attendant?"

She nodded yes.

"This is the real thing," I said.

The captain said in a calm manner, "If we need to evacuate, the signal will be ___. Do not use the exits which I call out. The floor lighting system will go on automatically. You will probably hear scraping noises when we land. I need Colleen up here in a couple of minutes to give her the emergency information."

Bradley, the other non-working flight attendant and I, gathered in the back of the aircraft. She was not in uniform but asked if there was anything she could do. I thanked her and said if we needed her we'd let her know.

The captain made an announcement to the passengers. He was awesome! He made it sound as though it was pretty much routine. "Ladies and gentlemen, if I could have your attention: We have a minor hydraulic problem and will be returning to Dallas. You will see some emergency rescue vehicles meeting us on the runway, but I don't expect there to be any problems."

Meanwhile, while Colleen was in the cockpit, I proceeded to the window exit rows to brief the passengers on how to open the exits. Before we take off, it is mandatory we ask each person in the exit row if they are willing and able to open the exits in case of an emergency. They always nod their head yes. Now, it was the real deal. Because of the light load, there were only four passengers to brief, three males and one female. Each was sitting on the aisle seat.

I stood in the aisle trying to project a calm demeanor.

"Does everyone know how to open these window exits in case of an emergency?"

I got four immediate responses. NO!

I continued, "Do not open the exits if you see any fire, debris or smoke. If you do, go to the nearest exit door and get out."

I pointed to the nearest door. I didn't want to alarm them, so I made sure I told them this was for precaution only. "I am sure everything will be fine."

I showed them the proper hand placement on the window. After opening the window, you will lay it on the seat. When on the wing, someone needs to help the people out. Follow the arrows on the wing to exit. Send the people away from the aircraft.

"Are there any questions?"

They shook their heads no.

"Again, this is only for precaution."

I went to the back of the aircraft. Colleen came out of the cockpit and joined us. We looked at each other for a second. Of course, what we really wanted to do was freak out, but we knew that would not be good. So being the professional flight attendants we were trained to be, we contained our emotions and got down to business.

We went over our commands for opening the emergency exits on our Super-80 aircraft. "At least you guys don't have to open the back of the plane's exit," Bradley said. He was right: it is the worst door to operate of all of the aircrafts. It is downright scary. After opening the door, you have to walk out on a metal walkway for about six steps to see if indeed the slide had deployed, if not, you have to pull the manual inflation handle to blow the slide.

As the three of us were going over our commands, adrenalin kicked in. Colleen and I had simple commands: "Jump, don't take anything with you. Jump, don't take anything with you." Bradley's commands were lengthy and more confusing. Because of our adrenalin high, we laughed as we all went blank on his commands. After a few attempts at remembering, we finally got it right. "Stay on your feet, jump into the slide, don't take anything with you. Stay on your feet, jump into the slide, don't take anything with you."

The captain came on the PA one last time. "Flight attendants, prepare for landing." We did our safety checks in the cabin. This time I was extra careful in checking to make sure all bags were under the seat and that absolutely nothing was in the bulkhead section on the floor.

I made my way to the exit rows. There, the young lady with her professional business attire was trembling with tears running down her cheeks. I told her everything will be all right. I gave her some tissues and again said, "We will be fine."

I sat down on my jumpseat with trepidation and put the seatbelt harness around my shoulders, making sure the safety belt was snug around my waist. I glanced at the flight attendant in the passenger seat. She had both feet planted on the floor with her hands placed on her thighs as if she were sitting on the jumpseat. I winked at her and asked if she would be my assistant in case of an evacuation. She nodded yes.

Studying the exit door next to me, I mentally ran thru my evacuation procedures. My hand placement for opening that particular door would be palms down to grasp the handle, turn to the right and rotate. I observed the little window on the door. I would look out first to see if any fire or smoke is visible before opening. I would then locate the handle on the aircraft which I was to grab to keep me from being pushed out of the aircraft when passengers' exited. A curtain was stuffed in the handle, so I removed it. I sat there trying not to think about the Sioux City airplane that cartwheeled and crashed in a field because of its hydraulic problem.

Glancing out the window, I of course said my prayers. I signaled to Bradley, (whose jumpseat was located where there was no outside view), that we were getting close to landing. I lowered my hand to the floor to show him we were about to touch down and then put both hands on my lap just as we were trained. I took a deep breath, put my faith in the pilots, and started to run the evacuation commands through my head.

We landed with the back gear touching down first. The captain took a while in lowering the nose gear. I felt as if we were doing a wheelie there for a while. When the nose gear lowered on the runway, I heard a grinding noise beneath me, but it didn't sound horrible. We continued speeding down the runway with emergency vehicles escorting us.

I looked at Bradley sitting in his jumpseat and excitedly gave him a high-five in the air. He gave one to me. I looked at the flight attendant next to me and gave the high-five sign as well. She returned the gesture. I then gave out a huge sigh of relief.

I knew we were not out of the woods until we came to a complete stop and there was no sign from the cockpit to evacuate.

After stopping the aircraft and hearing no signals, I finally began to relax.

Because of our hydraulic situation, there was no power to steer the aircraft. The landing gear doors are supposed to re-tract on their own but couldn't without power, that is why we heard the grinding noise. For some reason, it took nearly an hour to get a tug to where we were located on the runway.

After everyone deplaned from the aircraft, Bradley, Colleen and I walked in the terminal. "Look at our aircraft," Colleen said. I took pictures of our disabled landing gear. I told Colleen and Bradley I was glad they were with me on this flight because we all stayed calm and did exactly what we were supposed to do. The pilots did a wonderful job and again reflect on how important our annual training is to us.

At the beginning of the flight, I remember looking down at the entrance door and seeing a dime. I also thanked my guardian angel.

59

The Glam Job

Ah, the month of December; full airplanes filled with passengers cramming their luggage, Christmas packages, and heavy winter coats in the overhead bins. The weather delays are abundant because of the frequent de-icing procedures, heavy snowfall or foggy conditions. December means holidays which I just love but it also means cold and flu season. Delays and full planes are a given, but what really gets me is when people fly when they are very sick. You know; fever, coughing, sneezing, contagious, flu sick.

After we took off from West Palm Beach, Kim, our coach galley flight attendant, was setting up the beverage cart for our service. When she was finished, we maneuvered the cart in the aisle (which by the way weighs more than 200 pounds.) A female passenger tapped me on the shoulder. "I need to use the restroom right now," she whispered. We quickly returned the cart in the galley for her to pass by.

After completing our service, I was eating an apple in the galley. I glanced to my left and saw the same lady drop to the floor next to me. I immediately grabbed her to break her fall. She was still conscious.

I yelled, "Kim, help me lift her in the empty seat." I put the air vent on her pale face and asked if she was on any medication.

She said in a whisper, "I have the flu." First her daughter was contaminated, and then her husband, and now it was her turn. *I wondered who would be next.*

I put a cold cloth on her forehead. She looked at me with an alarmed look and said, "I think I am going to be sick." I quickly grabbed a barf bag from the seatback pocket and asked Kim to hand me a big silver bag that we use to pick up trash in the cabin. As I opened the barf bag to give to the woman, she vomited immediately. She was too fast for me to pull my hands away and threw up on my hands as well as in the bag.

The restrooms were all occupied as I gazed at my fingers spattered with vomit. I won't go into the smell. I quickly grabbed vodka from the liquor drawer and poured it all over my forearms, hands and fingers.

The very next flight from Chicago to Dallas, another female passenger, probably in her early 20's, stopped us in the middle of the aisle. "I don't feel very well; I need to get by."

This time I yelled at Kim, "GET THE CART BACK IN THE GALLEY NOW!" I didn't want to get puked on twice in the same day!

While we continued with our service, Kim went to check on the passenger in the restroom. She returned to me horrified. The young girl threw up in the sink, and it was filled to the brim. *Why didn't she thrown up in the toilet?* Kim said she locked off the lavatory.

The line was getting rather long during the flight with only one lavatory available (thanks to our sick passenger). If it were me, I would have had the courtesy to at least clean up my own mess. I did check on her during the flight and offered some ice chips. I wanted to say to her in a nice way that toilets flush, sinks do not, but I kept my mouth shut.

Toward the end of the flight, the sick girl was next in line for the lavatory. I needed to wash my hands, so I waited until she came out. I walked in and just about gagged. The sink was completely full again. She did not even attempt to drain it. We had to close the only remaining coach restroom. Luckily, it was time to land.

Upon arrival in Dallas, the cleaners entered the aircraft from the back stairs. "Which one of you lucky guys gets to clean the lavatories?" I chuckled.

He opened the restroom door and at least had a sense of humor about it. "Oh, she had pizza for lunch, he said jokingly. No, I think it was rice and beans."

Of course, he loved the reaction Kim and I gave him, "Eeeew."

On the very next trip, I was welcoming passengers aboard standing in front of the cockpit door. The first officer excused his way through so he could do his routine walk around. (Before every departure, one of the pilots does a safety check that includes walking around the airplane, checking for anything abnormal.)

After completing the job, the first officer passed by me again and sat down in the right seat of the cockpit. While I was still welcoming everyone onboard, I heard him say, "What is on my sleeve?" I glanced in the cockpit. A huge brown spot dotted his white shirt. Instinctively, he rubbed it with his hand and smelled it. He yelled out, "It's crap! I have crap on my shirt." He looked on his seat and there it was also. A big, brown gooey stain on the sheepskin cockpit seat!

At first we couldn't believe it. Who could have done such a thing? How could this have happened? I gave him some napkins soaked in club soda, but I jokingly assured him I wasn't going to clean him up.

Needless to say, we took a very long delay while our maintenance team tried to locate another cockpit seat cushion. The captain and first officer weren't going to smell that for the whole trip.

An hour passed and emotions calmed down a bit. After getting over the shock of it all, we realized the first officer must have stepped too close to the lavatory dump truck during his walk around. The sewage must have splashed on him while they were draining the toilets. When he sat down in the seat, his shirt rubbed against the cushion. We all got a good laugh on that one!

I went to use the restroom a little later. I opened the door and there lay a puddle of urine on the floor near the stool. *Why can't men aim directly in the toilet?*

"Ahh yes, what a glamorous job!"

60

Memory Lapse

$\mathscr{O}$ne great benefit with our job is the flexibility of trading, dropping, or picking up trips from other flight attendants. I received a phone call from a fellow crew member the day before my two-day, Friday-Saturday trip that was flying out of West Palm Beach. She had a two-day trip flying out of Miami on the same days as mine but didn't feel like driving all the way down there, so she asked if I would be interested in trading. Her trip had only one leg to Las Vegas and one leg back to Miami the next day, scheduled to arrive at 1:30 p.m. My two-day trip was much harder, flying three legs the first day with a later scheduled arrival of 6 p.m. on Saturday. Miami airport takes me about two hours and ten minutes to drive. Palm Beach airport takes me a little more than an hour. After careful deliberation, (especially being home earlier) I said I would trade with her.

The next day I was going to give myself plenty of time because Interstate 95 can be an absolute disaster with accidents and incidents. I made it all the way down to Fort Lauderdale when the weather turned for the worse. I slowed down as the rain pelted my windshield. The traffic began to crawl at a snail's pace. I was thankful I had given myself plenty of time, making it to the employee parking lot in two and a half hours.

The employee parking lot has many bus stops. I like the first stop so I am sure to get a seat. I was first to arrive with my umbrella in hand, waiting for the bus to come. Soon, from every direction the area became crowded with pilots, mechanics, airport employees and flight attendants. I kept looking at my watch waiting with anticipation. I'm not sure if it was because of the weather, but the bus was running late. By the time it came, anxious airport employees swarmed the bus ahead of me. I suddenly was reminded why I don't like to fly out of Miami. By the time the bus reached the fourth stop, it was completely full; everyone who was getting on had to stand for the ten minute ride to the airport.

There, I sat staring at a mob of people's behinds and crotches. You can tell everyone is staring at each other until they are caught and suddenly look away. A girl I hadn't seen for a while sat in the distance, but I really didn't feel like talking, so it was easier to pretend she wasn't there. The entire ride I was thinking I should have "princess parked." That means you just pay for parking at the airport and avoid the remote employee lot. As I glanced out the window I noticed the dark, ominous clouds coming our way. *I hope that is not going to affect my flight today.*

I signed in for my trip in operations, also checking to see if we had an on-time departure. Our arriving airplane was coming in early, so it looked as though everything was running smoothly.

I cleared security and headed to my gate. As I was sitting near the departure area, waiting for the arrival of our airplane, I noticed the rapidly approaching clouds. The skies darkened and at the same moment it was as though someone had dimmed the lights in the airport. The lighting struck at the same time the thunder roared. It was quite frightening. I was thankful I was on the ground as opposed to in the air.

The flight attendants who were working with me soon arrived at the gate. We were concerned about the weather when the agent confirmed our fears. The ramp was closed. What that means is all operations come to a halt. No airplanes will be taking off or landing, and no bags will be loaded or unloaded from the aircrafts. We did have some good news though. Our airplane had arrived and was waiting on the runway for the plane parked at our gate, to leave.

About an hour passed, and so did the first storm. The ramp opened up. I looked out the airport window at all the stranded jets. Workers were everywhere trying to make up for lost time. Baggage handlers were loading and unloading cargo, service guys were fueling the airplanes, and caterers were supplying the galleys.

One by one the planes rolled away from their gates. Our gate was now available for our aircraft's arrival. The agents ran down the jet bridge to open the door of the aircraft and let the passengers off. Of course the flight attendants love to people watch, so we critiqued everyone getting off the airplane. Judging by their attire, we guessed they were coming from a warm destination. We were right: it was Orlando.

After everyone deplaned and the aircraft was cleaned, the four of us moseyed onto the aircraft. It was now 5:50 p.m. Our scheduled departure was 4:50 p.m. As we were stowing our luggage in the overhead bin, a very hard lightning strike crashed as if it struck right next to the airplane. I jumped and even screamed it scared me so badly. The wind began to blow harder and harder; the empty aircraft swayed side to side. The agents came down to the airplane to let us know the ramp was closed again.

Meanwhile, the captain and first officer came aboard. I was in the back of the aircraft working as the number two galley flight attendant on our 757 aircraft. I saw the pilots talking to the other flight attendants in first class, so I joined them to introduce myself. When the captain saw me, he looked shocked. His eyes got big, his jaw dropped, and his open arms reached out to hug me. I cautiously hugged him back thinking this is a very touchy-feely kind of guy.

He was a tall, slender, nice-looking man. He spoke to me as if he knew me.

"I didn't think I would ever see you again and thought you might have quit," he murmured fondly.

I studied his face. "Raleigh?" I asked. Raleigh is where all the pilots and flight attendants were like family.

He said, "Yes".

We went back and forth asking about all the people we knew and their whereabouts. He looked vaguely familiar to me, but I just couldn't place him. I looked up his name on the paperwork. *Nope, nothing.* It didn't ring a bell. After all, that was more than twenty years ago.

He followed me to the back of the aircraft clearly wanting to talk more, but I needed to get busy. He seemed hurt that I wasn't more talkative and friendly and soon left to do his own pre-flight checks of the aircraft.

Another hour passed and soon the sky was clear enough for the ramp to open. Again the scurrying began as airplanes were loaded with bags, fuel and food. The agent started boarding the aircraft. The hustle and bustle of the outside workers was now replaced with the commotion of passengers finding a place for their luggage and nestling into their seats. Some were taking more time than others, but at this point everyone wanted to get away as soon as possible.

Finally, at 7:50 p.m. our 757 took off — three hours delayed. The flying time to Las Vegas is around five hours, which meant an arrival time of 12:50 a.m. EST. For someone who usually goes to bed around 9, this was not going to be an easy flight to work.

Many changes have occurred in my career as a flight attendant; this month brought yet another. Our airline was now going to be cashless. That is right: If you want a $2 headset, you better whip out that credit card. This was only my second trip using the credit card machine, so I was still getting comfortable with it. I knew a Vegas flight usually meant we have party animals who like to drink, so I was sure to get lots of practice.

For the most part passengers accepted the idea, but some were reluctant as they handed me their card. It seemed to take forever to do the service, though. Before, when someone handed us cash, we simply stuck it in our apron pocket and proceeded to the next customer. With a credit card, we swiped the card through a machine to document the sale. It's not difficult; it just takes a little more time.

Only one passenger gave me the run around. After making all appropriate announcements and making it clear several times, it was hard to misunderstand what we meant by credit/ debit cards only. As I approached this particular customer, I told my flight attendant partner, "I may have a problem with my next row."

She glanced at him with money in hand as we passed by with the cart. She nodded and said, "Good luck."

The male passenger had long, unwashed hair and a missing front tooth. I asked what he would like to drink.

He showed me his money, "I want two rum and Cokes."

I apologized to him for not being able to take his cash and explained once again, "We only take credit cards."

I saw his face getting red. "I don't have a credit card," he snapped.

I didn't want a fight on my hands. I gently but firmly told him, "I'll tell you what, since we just started this program I will give you these two drinks, but drink them slowly because that's all you're getting on this flight. Next flight, you must have a credit card."

He seemed pleased to receive his drinks for free, and I was pleased he hadn't caused a scene.

Only one other passenger tried to test me. "So what do I do if I want a sandwich, but I don't have a credit card?" I looked at her with my I guess you're out of luck face. After she realized she was not going to get a free sandwich, she pulled out her credit card.

After we finished our service, I continued to think of how I knew this captain. It was killing me! Due to the late hour, I was getting tired and was relieved when we heard the words, "Flight attendants, prepare for landing."

When everyone deplaned, I saw the captain briefing two of the other flight attendants. Their faces turned from weary to disbelief. I butted in on their conversation and asked what was going on. "We are reassigned for tomorrow. Because of our three-hour delay, we're going to be illegal to fly our one leg home to Miami." *Oh, great.* I guess getting in at 1:30 p.m. on a Saturday afternoon was not going to happen. Now instead we had to fly to New York in the morning, sit around for three hours, and then deadhead back to Miami arriving at 10:35 p.m. Needless to say, we were not happy. After printing out our new schedule and taking the bus ride to the hotel, we arrived in our rooms at 1:30 a.m. EST.

Morning came way to fast. Our pickup time was 6:10 a.m. Mountain time. At least I was able catch a good six hours of sleep. This particular hotel offered a free breakfast starting at 6 a.m. I went down early, not wanting to miss out. Everyone else on my crew had the same idea because we were all there enjoying our breakfast together trying to make light of what an awful trip this had been so far.

The flight attendants were at one table, and the captain and first officer were sitting next to us. I jokingly asked the captain, "Hey, did we have some kind of history together or what?" He just smiled and kept eating.

We all piled in the van that took us to the airport. After tipping the van driver for helping us with our luggage, the captain asked me to stay behind with him.

"I have something to tell you," he said. "A long time ago we were deadheading together in the back of the airplane. We were flirting heavily with each other. I pulled out a dollar from my wallet. I'll bet you this dollar that I can kiss you without touching you," he said he had told me. He recounted how he then leaned over and kissed me right on the lips.

I said, "Hey, you touched me."

To which he replied, "Here is your dollar." I laughed hysterically.

He also said he had a big crush on me back then. Wow! I blushed. *How could I not remember this? What else don't I remember?*

One of the main reasons I wrote this book is because a wonderfully wise, captain friend of mine wanted me to tell him some stories. I told him I received a speeding ticket that morning and wasn't in the mood to tell stories. He said, "Chris, do yourself a favor; buy a notebook and start writing your stories down because one day you are going to forget." I purchased a notebook the following week and started writing my stories down and years later, I have this book. Now I see what he was talking about. This was a perfect example of having one of those memory losses.

I looked at the captain differently. Perhaps he now got the look he hoped for when he first saw me the day before. I told him, "Hey, thanks for the memory."

During the entire New York flight I wanted to curl up somewhere and go to sleep. The thought of deadheading to Miami kept me going because I knew I could rest on that flight. I am sure the pilots were getting tired, but being New York based, they were home.

This was actually a much easier leg to work because all the passengers were catching up on their sleep from their activities in Vegas. Once again the sound of our captain's voice was fondly heard over the PA system, "Flight attendants, prepare for landing."

After sitting around two and a half hours in the New York airport, we boarded a 767 to take us to Miami. After having such an awful trip, we were delighted to see the agent had given us first class seats. This 767 was a newly configured aircraft which had reclining sleeper seats. I had never seen such airplane opulence.

As I took my seat, I felt like a passenger who was experiencing first class for the first time. *I wonder what this button is for. Hmmm, what is this other one for?* I opened up my pillow and blanket enclosed in plastic. I was surprised it was a luxurious down comforter. *This must be where our airline's money is going, I mused.* I didn't care. At that moment, I just wanted to snuggle comfortably under this lovely blanket. After we took off, I figured out what all the buttons meant and reclined my seat to ecstasy. I was conked out for the duration of the flight.

Two hours went by, when I was unhappily awakened by a different captain's voice. "Uh, ladies and gentlemen, Miami is experiencing a great deal of thunderstorms; we're going to prepare the cabin early for landing. Flight attendants, prepare for landing."

I was still half asleep when suddenly the plane jerked back and forth. We could hear the rain pounding against the fuselage. *Not again!* This time I WAS in the air. The flight attendant next to me instinctively grabbed her armrest. The first class passengers were probably not too comforted by that. But we are also human. My hands began to sweat. The back of the airplane is always worse in turbulence. *If it was bad where we were, what was it like there?*

The lightening cracked outside our window so brightly it blinded us. The boom of thunder heard was nerve racking. I often wonder why we have to fly through such weather. The plane took a sudden drop that caused the passengers to let out a gasp. I looked anxiously at the flight attendant sitting next to me. She responded with the same look. As always, I found myself saying some heavy-duty prayers.

Once again, I was greatly relieved when the wheels finally touched the runway. As we were taxiing to the gate the captain's voice came on the PA and said exactly what I did not want to hear, "The ramp is closed, ladies and gentlemen." We all let out a moan. All four of us deadheading flight attendants stared at each other in disbelief. It was now 10:53 p.m.

Luckily, it wasn't too much longer when we pulled in at the gate. I walked as fast as I could to get to the employee bus. Again the bus was late, and again the employees kept coming. When the bus finally arrived, the employees rushed the bus and all common courtesy was gone. I had to bully my way on and took the first available seat I could find.

Apparently, we weren't the only ones who had a bad day. I was surrounded by four very loud Spanish speaking gate agents who were extremely theatrical, one sitting to my right, one sitting to my left, and two standing directly in front of me.

I sat in my own little world as they jabbered on for the whole bus ride as if I weren't there.

One of my crew was sitting across from me. She made eye contact with me and knew exactly what I was thinking and burst out laughing. One of the agents caught on and said they had a lot of things happen to them that day. I told him I knew the feeling and everything is fine.

At 1:30 a.m., almost in a comatose state, I pulled my car in the driveway. It was exactly twelve hours later from when I was supposed to arrive. My Saturday was gone; however, I did gain a memory.

61

Snapped

First class used to be my favorite cabin to work. I felt like a hostess at my own little party and I enjoyed conversing and serving the passengers. One flight, many years ago, that carefree attitude all changed. I have heard many customers complain of bad flights due to rude flight attendants. My story is the exact opposite and it involves an incredibly rude passenger that affected me for years.

There are only a few little things that I don't enjoy about my job: I am uncomfortable cutting in line through security to work my flight. I don't really care for hanging up heavy coats (especially long, furry ones) in the wintertime. Lastly, and the one I enjoy least, is taking passengers food preferences in first class.

On each flight, the flight attendants are given a cart filled with trays, one for each passenger expected in first class. Passengers usually have a choice for their main entrée, such as barbeque chicken salad or a roast beef sandwich. Unfortunately, everyone may not get their first choice.

Our airline's standard procedure is to take preferences on an even flight number starting with the forward part of the cabin. On odd numbered flights we start from the back. This particular flight was an even-numbered breakfast flight.

After takeoff, I began preparation for my service by starting the coffee and getting my hot towels ready to go. Then, beginning with the front row, I asked each passenger if they would prefer corn flakes served with a banana and blueberries or a cheese omelet. On this flight, everyone wanted the omelets, which left only the cereal for the last row.

Passengers in 6A and 6B took it gracefully; however, the businessman sitting in 6E, threw an absolute tantrum. "What do you mean you are out of omelets? I am on a special diet and I need protein." (This is when the Atkins Diet was the latest craze.) He continued throwing his hands up in the air. "I can't believe this. I paid good money to sit up here and I WANT MY OMELET!"

I studied this grown man with his eyebrows deeply furrowed having an absolute meltdown in my cabin. "I do have warm bagels to serve."

He quickly snapped back, "Bagels are NOT protein!" After a long pause, he then spit out, "I will take the cereal!"

I looked at him blankly then turned and asked the passenger in 6F if he would be eating. He quickly nodded his head yes.

I entered my galley and said under my breath, "That is it; I will never work first class again!"

I avoided working first class for years. Flight attendants often called me to switch trips with them. My first question asked, "What cabin are you working?" If it was the number one position, I told them no way.

In January 2012 it happened. I messed up my bidding for the following month and mistakenly pressed the number 1 key on the computer for my position selection.

A few days later I checked to see what I held for February, and there it was in black and white: Selection 142, Position 1. It had to be a mistake; the scheduling department must have screwed up. No way would I have bid number one. After a period of denial, the reality sunk in. I must have made the wrong position selection when bidding.

I dreaded working the following month like the plague. Many changes occurred up front during the years I had avoided serving the first class cabin. I used to work on a Super-80 and now I was going to work a brand new 737 aircraft. Instead of reading from a PA card to brief passengers, an automated message delivered it for us. I simply had to queue it up and hit the right buttons. All the new gadgets were a little intimidating for me.

Attached to a wall is a control panel we use to program our flight. We simply input the flight number and flying time in the device, and it makes all of our announcements for us. A woman's voice speaks softly as she makes the seatbelt PA, exit row announcements and the safety briefing about the 737. This is a wonderful concept as long as it works. Because of all the unpredictable glitches, though, we have named this system Sybil. Sometimes she does not take directions well and will not work.

So in the week prior to first class service I prepared myself as best I could mentally. How hard could it be? I was lucky to have my good friend Donna working with me, so that made me feel a little bit better.

On that dreaded day, I drove to the airport an hour early hoping to get on the airplane and study the first class galley. It was a morning flight out of West Palm Beach where there is no catering facility. That means the food was brought in on a flight the night before and stored in an air-conditioned room. That also meant there would be only one entree to serve, which was cereal. To eat or not to eat, that was the question.

As I entered the airplane, I immediately eyeballed Sybil. She looked innocent enough. I checked the emergency equipment to make sure it was there. I unwrapped the cereal into the bowls. Then I realized it was like riding a bike. My previous years of setting up the galley came flooding back to me.

Eventually the crew came on and asked why I was on the airplane so early. I explained the situation, and it got a good laugh. The captain pulled me aside to brief me about the flight.

I still felt a little unsure, especially while imputing the information into Sybil. I tested out the system, and it worked fine. Throughout the boarding process, Sybil's voice was heard informing everyone the correct placement for their luggage. Working in coach for so long, I forgot what it was like to say "welcome" to everyone coming on board.

After all passengers were seated and the overhead bins were shut, the agent closed the door. "Ladies and gentlemen the agent has closed the forward door," I announced. "Turn off all electronics and cell phones at this time; anything with an on and off button needs to be turned off. Flight attendants prepare your doors for departure and cross check." (Believe it or not, I had successfully avoided working first class since the incident with the businessman, pre-dating the cell phone era, which means I never had given an electronic or cell phone PA)! I told the captain how many passengers we had on board and closed the cockpit door.

The aircraft pulled away from the gate. Palm Beach airport doesn't have a lot of airplanes taking off at the same time, so it is usually a short taxi before takeoff. I made a welcome announcement with the flying time and weather for D/FW. I then pushed Sybil's button to give the safety briefing about our 737 aircraft. I waited and waited and thought, "Come on Sybil, not *this* morning." But she wasn't awake yet and decided not to speak. Knowing I didn't have much time, I quickly called the other flight attendants to retrieve the equipment needed to manually brief our passengers. Panicking, I retrieved my PA card out of my bag as the other flight attendants stood in position with seatbelt in hand.

"Ladies and gentlemen, we ask that you give your attention to your flight attendants as they brief you about the 737 aircraft." I took a deep breath and calmly read the instructions. It was amazing how the announcements came right back to me, somehow etched in my mind from years of practice.

The service went beautifully as Donna and I worked together with poise and professionalism. I enjoyed it immensely as I felt it was my own little party again. Two passengers gave us thank you cards for excellent service.

Looking back, I realized I should not have let one rude passenger's immature behavior affect me so much. Remember, the next time you are flying to be kind to your flight attendants; they are trying to do their job as best they can.

62

A Walk in My Heels

Exhausted! Why am I so exhausted? Maybe it's because I have just worked three legs across the country over a fourteen hour day on hardly any sleep.

Passengers talk to me all the time about other flight attendants and other airlines. It's no surprise that they measure the airlines by the quality of the flight attendants and their flying experience with those crews. Oh, Southwest airlines flight attendants are this. Well, Delta's flight attendants are ___, American's flight attendants are____, etc., etc. Here is the bottom line: We are all pretty much the same, just *plane* tired.

A flight attendant's job is largely dictated by their seniority. When we are first hired, junior flight attendants are placed on reserve. Everyone pays their dues. As the company hires more flight attendants, we are eventually bumped off the reserve list. There was a lull in hiring which stagnated seniority for an entire population of flight attendants, holding them on indefinite reserve until hiring resumed.

As our seniority increases, we are able to hold better trips. Every month we submit a bid sheet for the following month. We select positions, sign-in times, layover destinations, and our days off. Early in my career, I would dream about all those low stress senior trips. For example, one leg to sultry Puerto Vallarta in the morning and have the whole day to relax. The next day all you had to fly was one leg back to Dallas. I'm sure the flight attendants working those flights were happy and had plenty of smiles to go around. Well, those days are gone and those cushy layovers are pretty much nonexistent — at least where I am based.

Before 9/11, we negotiated a contract that pleased everyone. The flight attendants had received a pay raise and enhancements to work rules and benefits. We were all so excited to participate in our company's success! For three months, we were able to enjoy that raise. Flight attendants were buying the homes they could now afford. Some were upgrading their old cars for new ones.

After 9/11, it was taken away from us. Most people were afraid to fly, leaving the airline industry suffering as the planes were taking off with fewer and fewer passengers. Our company was desperately trying to stay solvent along with everyone else. Some airlines had to claim bankruptcy. In order for us to avoid that, we had to cut expenses across the board. The flight attendants had to give up our new contract and then some or we too would have to file for bankruptcy. We begrudgingly accepted those cuts with the understanding that when the company got back on its feet, we would eventually get back what we had given up. We not only said goodbye to our pay raise, but took a significant pay reduction. The work rules dramatically changed. Our days got longer and our vacation days got shorter.

If you have ever flown, you know what it is like to have jetlag. Just because we fly for a living doesn't mean we are immune. After a long day on the airplane with recycled air, the flight attendants have red eyes and a sallow complexion. I call it "the pasties" because we all look kind of pale. After a typical three-day trip, I am basically on the couch the next day recovering from jetlag.

The frequent changes in air pressure has an effect on us also. Have you ever seen a potato chip bag during a flight? It expands and gets hard as a rock. Or, have you ever had the unpleasant experience of opening a container of yogurt while flying? It explodes all over you. Now you know where all that gas is coming from! After I get home from a trip, my stomach looks pregnant. One can only imagine what that is doing to our bodies.

When I was single, I was asked to participate in a study comparing our occupation to a teachers. My understanding was that a high rate of miscarriages and fertility problems amongst flight attendants had come to the attention of a health organization. They wanted to gather some relevant data including how much radiation we were exposed to while flying. For one month, I wore a device similar to a watch that detected and reported radiation. I also had to spit in a tube every morning and freeze it. I never saw the results but I am still curious about them and the study.

The turbulence has been noticeably awful in recent years. I have found myself thrown onto a passenger's lap on more than one occasion. When I get home from trips, my husband is always asking how I got this or that bruise. It is always due to turbulence. We are constantly being thrown about the galley and bounced around in the aisles. I know of flight attendants who have hit the ceiling during the flight. Some have become unconscious or have broken bones because of it.

One other strain worth mentioning is lifting bags into the overhead bin. Lugging our own bags from employee parking lots, thru security, from gate to gate, into the bins and onto vans to the hotels is plenty for all of us. So don't take it personally if when you ask for help with your bag, you catch a bit of an attitude from the flight attendant. Sure I lend a hand, I am a sucker for kids and little old ladies who need help, but what I really want to say is, "Honey, next time please check your bag."

One of our work rule legalities that changed was lengthening our day from a twelve hour maximum day to a fifteen hour maximum day. Our minimum layover time was shortened to eight hours. It usually takes me about fifteen minutes to wash my face, put my pajamas on, and hop into bed. I set my alarm an hour and fifteen minutes before my pick-up time. If I went to sleep right away, that would only give me six and a half hours of sleep.

In the old days, we were allowed to reward our frequent flyers with a to-go bag full of liquor miniatures. They loved it! It made them feel appreciated. When I was on a long flight or one that was delayed in the air, I often played a game over the PA with the passengers. I'd ask, "Does anyone have a paper clip in their bag? Who has ten or more one dollar bills with them?" etc. etc. Whoever won got a bottle of champagne or wine. Those days are gone. No more giveaways. I understand these are different times and conditions. But when people say it is not the same, I relate because it is not the same for us either.

We have to absorb and roll with a lot of interesting passenger behavior and constantly contain our emotions and feelings.

If someone treats us badly, vents their flying frustrations on us, or say a situation is our fault, we have to address it professionally and take it; that is our job. The pressure has gone up, longer hours in the air, lower pay, more responsibility and a lot less fun and glamour.

You may want to factor some of this in before coming to a harsh conclusion about the flight attendants serving you. Some of us are morning people like me. I don't mind early morning trips at all. Now, I turn into a pumpkin around seven o'clock at night. My energy is gone and my smiles are a bit forced.

I am not making any excuses for unprofessional behavior by flight attendants. I'm just saying that it's a challenging job and for the most part, the good old days are gone for us also. I believe the vast majority of the flight attendants are hardworking, committed employees that care about the passengers and their fellow crewmembers and work very hard to make your flying experience as smooth and enjoyable as possible.

63

Just the Facts

- More than 25,000 planes take off every day in the U.S.
- Traveling at cruising altitude, the temperature outside the airplane is 43 – 80 degrees below zero.
- A 737 aircraft weighs approximately 96,300 pounds. The maximum loaded weight is 174,400 pounds.
- A 737 airplane typically travels at 31,000 – 37,000 feet, 7 miles above sea level. The highest altitude for a 737 to travel is 41,000 feet. (Other aircrafts may fly higher.)
- One minute of flying is approximately one automobile tank of gas (1,000 gallons per hour). Commercial airplanes use a formula of pure kerosene with antifreeze for jet fuel.
- A flight from New York to Los Angeles is about 2,100 nautical miles. A 737 burns roughly 2.5 gallons of fuel per mile. (About 5,000 gallons coast to coast.)
- Airplane engines have built in fire extinguishers.

- It is impossible to open the door in a pressurized cabin.

- Static in the air can cause purple and blue streaks on the cockpit window that resembles lightening. This is known as St. Elmo's fire.

- Depending on the aircraft, a commercial jet's speed on approach for landing is approximately 130 – 175 mph. The takeoff speed is around 140 – 175 mph.

- The standard separation of airplanes in flight is 1,000 vertical feet.

- On approach to an airport, airplanes generally are separated by 5 miles. As they get closer to the runway, the gap narrows to 30 seconds apart.

- A main landing gear tire on a 737 aircraft cost about $2000 – $2500. They last for approximately 150 landings before they need to be replaced.

- In most airplanes, pilots steer on the tarmac with their feet. Some aircraft have tillers for steering.

- In an emergency evacuation, it takes one second per passenger to evacuate the aircraft (as long as everyone complies to leave their stuff behind).

64

Soldier Bob

*E*very time uniformed military personnel come aboard, I always welcome them with a pat on the shoulder and a simple phrase, "Thank you for serving." It was always said with heartfelt sincerity, I thought, until I got a wakeup call from a soldier named Bob.

Before a trip begins — usually on the way to the airport — I often say my prayers. On this day, I said a prayer and asked, "If there is someone you would like me to talk to on the flight, please send them my way."

After my first class service was complete, I was busy in the galley cleaning up. A man probably in his late 30s poked his head in and said, "I am glad the company I work for switched airlines because I really enjoyed watching the two of you do your job." His seat was in the first row of coach, but he could observe the first class service from where he was sitting. Now I will have to admit I was preoccupied with my galley, but there was something about him that urged me to talk to him. About that time, Angie, the other first class flight attendant, stepped around the corner. The mannerly young man felt in the way and gracefully left the galley. Before he could leave, I remembered my prayer and gently grabbed his arm and ushered him to a private spot next to the exit door.

He began by saying, "I used to be in the military."

"Did you serve over in Iraq," I questioned.

"Yes," he said. "I was shot two times in the stomach." He pointed to where he had been wounded. I noticed one of his ears was disfigured, perhaps due to another combat injury. There was a hearing aid in his other ear. He noticed me looking at him and said, "I am partially deaf now, but I can read lips." He showed me his wrist where his hand was severed but was surgically reattached. I took a deep breath knowing this was going to be quite the conversation.

"Do you have post-traumatic stress disorder?" I asked.

"Oh yeah," he replied. "All of us who were witnesses to anything severe have it. I saw thirteen of my troop lost." He continued, "I was a sniper. I was posted on top of a building monitoring activities on the ground. One day, I saw a young boy who was obviously handicapped being lead into the middle of the street. I remember saying to myself, oh no, no, no. Then I witnessed and heard the explosion. Someone had placed a bomb around this helpless child and executed him." In stunned silence, I swelled with sympathy and gazed at Bob. He continued, "The next time, a woman was escorted out into the street. Again I said, oh no, no, no…"

Many of us have been traumatized by a single incident in our lives and it takes us years to adjust. The horror that many of our young men, many barely 19 or 20 years old, saw while serving is literally unimaginable for most of us.

Bob went on to explain, "What compounds issues for many returning veterans, whether they are mentally or physically challenged or not, is the fact that decent jobs are hard to find. A friend of mine who couldn't find work committed suicide, another sits at home on the couch day and night drinking himself to death. It is a real problem."

I told him how sorry I was, and that it was an honor and privilege to have met him.

On my flight the next day, a uniformed soldier boarded the aircraft. Now as I spoke the words, "Thank you for your service," they had much more meaning. A first class seat was empty, so Angie and I upgraded him. He was a handsome young man who like so many of our troops was mannerly and gracious. He favored a young Leo Dicaprio. He was so exhausted he slept during the entire flight.

As I was serving the women next to him, she whispered to me, "Do you always upgrade the military?"

I said, "We do what we can for them. If they are in coach, we give them something to eat for free."

As her eyes filled with tears, she looked fondly at the sleeping soldier, "He is someone's baby boy."

"I know," I said sadly. I smiled at her as I too was getting weepy. I went to the restroom to grab some tissues for the woman who now had tears streaming down her face. We shared a helpless nod as I handed the Kleenex to her.

65

Post Traumatic Turbulence Syndrome

$\mathscr{P}$TTS. Post Traumatic Turbulence Syndrome. There really isn't such a disorder, but there should be. I have experienced many severe turbulence events which has deeply affected me.

In April of 2009, we started our flight from Miami to Houston with good weather. About an hour and a half remained of the flight when the captain called back and said there were indications from planes ahead of us that we were going to be in for quite a ride. He asked us to go ahead and put everything away and lock up the galley.

We were flying on a 737 aircraft. The tail of a 737 is known to zigzag a bit especially during turbulence. Andrea and I took our jumpseats early because the light turbulence turned to moderate chop. We continued to read our magazines, the airplane jolting us from side to side now and then as we read.

We received another call from the captain with about forty-five minutes to land. "Take your seats immediately," he commanded. We notified him we were already strapped into our jumpseats. The tone in his voice scared me.

Suddenly the aircraft began to thrash about. The plane dipped and tipped from side to side. Luckily, our jumpseats on this airplane are away from the view of passengers. Andrea and I looked at each other with fear in our eyes.

We went straight to severe turbulence. I grabbed the base of my jumpseat with my hands as it lifted from its brackets. With a thud, the jumpseat fell back into place. Usually in turbulence there are periods of calm in between jolts. Not this time. It continued on and on. Suddenly, the airplane just dropped (I don't know how many feet.) The 200-pound locked beverage carts simultaneously lifted into midair. When the pilot regained control, the carts came down in unison with a CLA-CLANG!

My hands still clutching the seat beneath me were now wet with perspiration. Again, the airplane dropped and the passengers screamed. I wanted to also. All we could do was sit there and take it.

The prayers flowed freely. "Please God; put your protective angels around the airplane." Again, another prayer, "Please calm the skies ahead." And yet another prayer, "Please forgive me of all my sins (especially the Rio de Janeiro days)." This was the first time in my career I thought we were going to crash due to turbulence.

As we got closer to Houston, rain pounded the aircraft and wind continued to jostle us about. One particular jolt popped open an overhead bin. It was within my viewing area, but there was no way I could stand up to close it. A passenger sitting below managed to reach up above his head to slam it shut. *Whew, thank God.* All we needed was luggage flying around.

A waft of vomit permeated the cabin. I couldn't look at Andrea because I was so full of fear. We were too afraid to speak. All I could do was close my eyes and pray to make the turbulence go away.

Finally, we heard the landing gear lower. The plane was still violently jerking us about. "Please help us God," my prayer continued. The wings were still going from side to side when we landed. The wheels touched not once, but twice. I let out a huge sigh of relief.

As passengers were deplaning, I could see that the turbulence had taken its toll on them as well. I told them there would be no extra charge for the roller coaster ride. They all laughed but we all knew how lucky we were to be safely on the ground. Three beautiful, young ladies were traveling together. I heard one of them say, "At least we would have gone down together." Everyone was pretty shaken, including the two of us. I can't imagine how the poor pilots landed in those conditions!

When we were on the van taking us to the hotel, I asked the captain what happened. He said the radar was completely red. There were no indicators to locate where the air pockets or cells were; "We just had to weather it," he said. The first officer was silent and simply sat with a look of exhaustion on his face. I am so grateful to that crew.

While still parked at the airport terminal, horns began to honk as traffic came to a halt. Our van driver was getting pretty angry, throwing his hands up in the air. I looked out the window and saw that our storm had now engulfed the airport. The driver said there were tornadoes spotted in the area. *We were flying through tornadoes! No wonder!*

We saw some activity ahead and traffic began to creep forward. Some barricades had been blown over by the wind, blocking the exit out of the airport. I shook my head in disbelief that we had just flown through that weather.

Throughout the year it seemed as though we were flying through storms every month. After a while, I started to become a nervous flier. At the first sign of turbulence, I immediately headed straight for my jumpseat and strapped in. Even if it was moderate chop, my hands would perspire.

Then it hit, Christmas Eve, 2009. Chicago to Austin. The captain, on each flight, is required to give a briefing to the number one flight attendant. On this particular flight, he requested that all of us attend. "Austin is reporting heavy storms and high winds today. I am going to have you take your seats a little early." *Uh oh, that's all I need!*

Later on in the flight, the captain was true to his words. Ding! Ding! "Okay you guys, we are starting our descent into Austin. Put everything away and take your seats after preparing the cabin for landing."

Before I was able to sit down, the plane went into severe turbulence. I quickly closed up my galley and carefully made my way to the jumpseat grabbing each passenger's headrest to maintain my balance. I plopped into my jumpseat and strapped on the harness. I was being whipped and tossed about as though I was riding a bucking bull in a rodeo. *"Good Lord,"* I murmured. *"Please make it stop."* But it didn't.

I wanted control — any control. Instinctively, my feet hit the floor as if I were trying to slam on the brakes. I flattened my hands against the walls surrounding the jumpseat to try and brace myself.

The plane dropped (along with my stomach) then slowly regained altitude. I felt as though I could throw up. (I have never been sick on an airplane.) Luckily, I was the galley flight attendant on a Super-80 aircraft, which meant no one could see me. The other flight attendant sat facing me about five rows up. She kept looking at me for some kind of reassurance; I had none to offer.

Hearing the landing gear lower was a welcome sound at this point. The plane jolted back and forth. I knew we would be touching down soon, but the wind shear was severe.

Hoping the flight would end soon, my heart sank when I heard the engines fire up to full throttle as the captain aborted the landing. Secretly, I wished we could land somewhere else, but all we did was circle around in the strong wind. Usually when this happens, the captain will make an announcement as to why the airplane is maneuvering. On this day, however, I think he was too busy flying to make any announcement.

I tried unsuccessfully to control my fear. I took two slow, even breaths to calm me down, which helped some. Finally, I heard the landing gear lower again. *Steady boys, bring 'er in.*

I looked at Samantha on the other jumpseat. She was in full view of passengers, her eyes wide open and easily readable. *What the heck is going on? Why aren't we landing?* She glanced out the window and then to me. We were tossed about until the wheels actually touched the ground. Even after contact with the runway, the fuselage dipped one last time.

After everyone deplaned, the captain told the number one flight attendant that was the most difficult landing of his entire career. A flight later that afternoon, also traveling from Chicago to Austin, actually hit the wing on the runway because of the high winds. The FAA was on the news saying they were going to do further investigation as to why it happened.

On a flight the following year, my good friend Donna and I, were given the command to take our seats immediately. We had just completed our beverage service and didn't have time to lock down the galley cabinet doors. Just after we strapped in, the plane dropped hundreds of feet. The unsecured inserts filled with juice, milk and cans of soda flew out of the shelves. Some of the soda cans exploded as they hit the floor. One of them landed squarely on my toe causing me to yelp in pain. I braced my hands against the galley counter and injured my right thumb. Customer call buttons chimed, alerting us to the chaos in the cabin. All of their beverages hit the ceiling. The cabin looked like a war zone littered with ice, cups, cans and trash. Everyone was wearing whatever they were drinking. And just like that it was over... The plane was a wreck and I felt the same.

A few years have passed since these events luckily with no further incidents of severe turbulence. I feel somewhat back to normal. I wear the seatbelt when I can and always quickly heed the captains warning to take my seat and fasten my seatbelt. Take it from me, you should too or you might be the next PTTS sufferer.

66

I've Learned…

$\mathcal{I}$ have been flying for over twenty-five years now. There have been thousands of flights and thousands upon thousands of interactions with every class, nationality, race and religion of people on this planet. That opportunity has taught me some valuable lessons, some of which I have shared already. I can't share every moment; however, this is what I can tell you:

- I've learned you can spread happiness to an unhappy person, but true happiness comes from within.
- I've learned the most powerful emotion people respond to is kindness.
- I've learned to always say thank you. Recognize and thank anyone who has prepared your meal, given or done something on your behalf or just give thanks for the sunrise and sunset.
- I've learned to ask for something you really want. Expecting others to read your mind is a mistake.

- I've learned you can tell a lot about a person by just looking at them but that you should not judge them.

- I've learned you can't look at a relationship to fulfill you, though the right partner will enhance your life.

- I've learned it is difficult to embrace change because we yearn for the familiar.

- I've learned a survivor emerges from adversity with a stronger spirit.

- I've learned intuition, your inner voice, your guardian angel and your gut feeling may all be connected.

- I've learned the power of prayer is real. All you have to do is ask.

- I've learned it is okay to dream big, but you have to appreciate where you are now.

- I've learned knowing there is someone with you at all times is empowering.

- I've learned expectations can only lead to disappointment.

- I've learned when I am at peace and in tune with my spirit, I am kind, patient, loving and generous. When I am not at peace, I am the exact opposite: unkind, impatient, unloving and selfish.

- I've learned the feeling of pure joy is rare and present when my life is balanced.

- I've learned it is better to find common ground with those with whom you disagree.

- I've learned in a healthy environment we thrive. In an unhealthy environment we wilt.

- I've learned the magic moments in life cannot be repeated. It is just that: a moment. Whether it is a fall festival you have attended, a tender moment within a relationship, or a special time in your life. That moment cannot be relived or recreated but can always be cherished.

- I've learned a smile is as contagious as a yawn.

- I've learned some people have difficult lives because *they* are difficult.

- I've learned one secret to living a long life is to mind your own business. Taking on the burdens and responsibilities of those around you takes a toll.

- I've learned there are those who enhance your mojo and there are those who drain it.

- I've learned it is easier to tell a story than to write one.

Epilogue

Flight attendants tell me all the time, "I lead a boring life compared to yours." I have wondered why they say this and have a few ideas.

There are many roads one can take through life. Straight roads get you where you want to go safely and predictably. The winding path usually includes risk, adventure and for me, a sense of endless possibility. I choose adventure every time, I think that is why I wanted to become a flight attendant in the first place.

People also frequently ask me, "Why are you so happy?" I cannot say for sure, but I think it is because I have been fortunate enough to find my purpose. Flying has enabled me to fulfill that purpose and be true to myself. I want to make a difference in people's lives. I enjoy putting a smile on someone's face and spreading good cheer.

My career as a flight attendant has been everything I hoped it would be and much, much more. Many interesting people have come my way; each on their own unique journey. As we crossed paths, I have enjoyed making those memorable and special connections.

My journey continues and I hope that if in the future your plans call for air travel, your trip is full of adventure and remember, *Fasten Your Seatbelts*!